Jayce Lu...

D0443475

THIRD and LONG

THIRD and LONG

NEIL LOMAX
with J. David Miller

Fleming H. Revell Company
Old Tappan, New Jersey

Scripture quotations in this book are from the King James Version of the Bible.

GV
939
.L59A3
1986

Library of Congress Cataloging-in-Publication Data
Lomax, Neil.
  Third and Long.

    1. Lomax, Neil.   2. Football players—United
States—Biography.   3. St. Louis Cardinals (Football
team)   4. Sports—Religious aspects—Christianity.
I. Title.
GV939.L59A3   1986   796.332′092′4   [B]   86-24830
ISBN 0-8007-1497-0

Copyright © 1986 by Neil Lomax
Published by the Fleming H. Revell Company
Old Tappan, New Jersey 07675
Printed in the United States of America

14·02 14G

Dedicated to my Lord and Savior Jesus Christ, my wonderful wife, Laurie, and my beautiful baby son, Nicholas Ryan.

I would like to acknowledge several friends for their help in this effort, including Coach Darrell "Mouse" Davis, the true king of the Run 'n' Shoot offense; the football Cardinals, particularly Greg Gladysiewski and Bob Rose; Leigh Steinberg, the best sports attorney of all time; Pastor Ron Kincaid, my lifelong spiritual leader and friend; the Lomax family, for their love and patience through the years; my brother Mitch, who will never really know his impact on my life; and David Miller (and his wife, Lisa), for his unselfish and dedicated work on this project, for without him, this book never would have been attempted.
Those wishing to correspond with me may do so by writing to:

Neil Lomax
c/o Pro Athletes Outreach
P.O. Box 1044
Issaquah, WA 98027

Praise His Name!

Neil Lomax

Contents

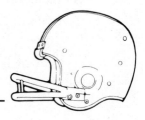

THIRD and LONG

1

When Glamour Hurts

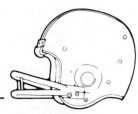

"The ultimate measure of a man is not where he stands in moments of comfort and convenience, but where he stands at times of challenge and controversy."

—Martin Luther King, Jr.

November 28, 1985, was an unusually cold, overcast afternoon in Texas Stadium, particularly for a Thanksgiving Day. The wind snapped at my cheeks as my St. Louis Cardinal teammates and I poured from the south end of the stadium amid a torrent of boos and catcalls, which resonated like a gutlike rumble from one end of the stadium to the other. Huddled fans, many adorned with cowboy hats, momentarily left the warmth of their blankets and bourbon to stand and release throaty roars of disapproval for me and my red-shirted comrades. That afternoon, the year-long misery of my difficult and even embarrassing fifth season as quarterback for the Cardinals came to a head.

A morning rain had left the artificial turf damp, and the added cold gave it the flexibility of Sheetrock. The firmness of the surface could be felt through my Nike turf shoes and up into my legs as I warmed up, but it didn't interfere with the crispness I felt in my right arm. Despite having won only four of twelve games all year, I still thought we had a chance to win. We hadn't been consistent throughout the season, and many outside distractions had thoroughly ruined what had appeared to be a promising year.

The previous season we'd won nine games and lost seven, missing the play-offs by two feet—the margin between kicker Neil O'Donoghue's winning 50-yard field goal attempt and the goalpost in the season finale against the Washington Redskins. My 4,614 yards passing was third-best in the history of National Football League quarterbacks, but was overshadowed by Dan Marino's all-time record of 5,084 yards the same year (San Diego's Dan Fouts produced 4,802 in 1981 and 4,715 in 1980). Nevertheless, our team's strong performance led experts to pick us to win the NFC East in 1985. Then the bottom fell out. We were one of the hardest-hit clubs in the league with an assortment of problems. Respect for the coaches was totally nonexistent, player relationships crumbled, and injuries were rampant. Before the season started we were full of confidence, but by midseason all hopes of play-off contention were dispelled as we braced ourselves for a long second half of the season.

It seemed like eternity before Thanksgiving rolled around. Funny thing about playing football—when you're winning, time flies; when you're losing, weeks feel like years. In the locker room before the Dallas game, there was this horrible feeling of "let's just get this thing over with." We still had a few pivotal ball games coming up against some teams that needed to beat us to get to the play-offs—including the Cowboys—but nobody seemed to care. My attitude, I admit, was hardly the best.

But I love playing against Dallas. As a kid, I used to fantasize about being quarterback for the Cowboys, Rams, or Packers, not realizing I would line up against these teams fifteen years later. Playing football against my brothers, Terry and Mitch, in the backyard of our home in Lake Oswego, Oregon, I always cast them in the role of some woebegone team while I was always the better team. I always won convincingly, largely because I played not only the team itself, but also the coach, the referees, the announcers, and the home crowd. I dreamed of being an NFL quarterback, of trotting off the field and huddling with coaches like Vince Lombardi and Tom Landry on the sidelines. Had I been able to foresee how my dream would come to pass, I might have had second thoughts.

Thus, playing against Dallas offered extra incentive. Besides, the wide-open, gambling defensive style of the Cowboys leaves no margin for error. Either they make a big play or you make a big play, and we'd had great success against them in the past. We had beaten them on "Monday Night Football" just four weeks earlier; in fact, it had been our last win. To sweep Dallas would have been a high note in a dismal season. I was well prepared, but I lacked the "oomph"—that confidence I'd felt in 1984. The all-around atmosphere in the locker room was different. Which strikes a point few people understand: Sure, we're highly paid to play a glamorous game, but when things get tough, we still want to win—despite the money, despite everything. Once you're into a game, the competitive juices begin flowing on their own, regardless of how hard you try to pretend you don't care. A true athlete whose heart is in his profession just can't stand the lackadaisical attitude that tends to set in when a team starts losing games.

The locker room before a game is like a bunker full of infantrymen prior to combat; in a sense, you are going to war. Spotless white medical tape is wound around and around ankles, knees, and wrists with surgical precision by skilled trainers. Liniment permeates the air with a hospital odor. Shots for pain are administered to the ailing. The intermittent clang of a locker door is heard over the normally low chitchat as players dress. The smell of bleach is evident on clean jerseys and pants, though a grass stain or turf burn leaves evidence here and there of the last violent engagement with the "other" guys.

I was dressed from the waist down when the footsteps of offensive coordinator Dick Jamieson came padding down the carpeted aisle. A very likable, rotund man with salt-and-pepper hair and a great sense of humor which I always admire in coaches, Dick had really suffered emotionally when the club began to slide. The frustration of the season showed in his face. The raccoonlike circles that lapped his eyes were evidence of his late-night dates with a whirring projector and hours of game film. With the team sinking, and fast, the way I performed had a direct impact on the duration of his job. In pro football, coaches are the first to go when a team can't snap a losing streak, and he knew he was getting closer and closer to the unemployment line.

"Neil," he said, crossing his arms and leaning against the locker, "let's make a little pact here. Let's finish these last four games strong. Starting today."

His eyes flashed fire, but I looked down at him blankly.

"C'mon, Dick," I sighed, struggling with my jersey as I pulled it over my head and pads, jiggling my shoulders to get a good fit before I tucked it into my tight, white nylon game pants. "You know I'm always loose, I'm always ready to play. I don't need a pep talk." I reached back inside my locker for a couple of wristbands.

"Don't give me any crap, Neil," Dick retorted, grabbing my arm—and my attention. "Let's go out and do our jobs the way we know we can. Forget everything else. Throw that ball like there's no tomorrow—have some fun."

A smile played slowly across my lips. I admired his determination not to just throw in the towel, as many of the other coaches had. And Dick showed me something. For the first time that year, I realized I'd been missing the boat all season. My aggravation with other players for whatever reasons—this guy's injury, that guy's attitude problem—had kept me from concentrating on my own game. I was getting knocked around (when we finished the year I had been sacked sixty-seven times, a team record no quarterback likes), but I was responsible for many of those. Roy

Green, an incredible wide receiver, had missed most the year because of nagging injuries, and that upset me; not having Roy took our speed and the "bomb" out of our offense. Roy, a black, six-foot, 195-pounder from Henderson State, began his pro career as a defensive back in 1979, then set new club receiving records and went to the Pro Bowl when he was switched to wideout in 1983. Talk about talented, Roy is a great athlete and a quick-witted, fun guy to be with. But with Roy hurt, Pat Tilley was having to carry the load as receiver, and at age thirty-three and just five-ten and 178 pounds, he spent most of the year getting hammered. Pound-for-pound, Pat is probably the toughest man I've ever seen. Fearless over the middle, relentless on the corners, Pat is brilliant at confusing a defensive back. But by Thanksgiving his small body had paid the price, and he was physically beaten. Yet he continued to play when others wouldn't, his will unbent, without complaint. If I had to define a true professional, Pat Tilley certainly fits that mold.

The tight ends were having a lousy year. The coaches were always on their back, saying they couldn't run-block, they couldn't pass-protect, and they couldn't catch the ball. One guy I really felt for at that position was Doug Marsh, who is one of the best but, like the rest of us, hadn't been able to put it together all year. The running back position was a revolving door, as well. O. J. Anderson, our huge and bruising, two-time All-Pro, hadn't played regularly because of injuries. Earl Ferrell, a tough fullback who in 1984 spared me from many blitzing linebackers, disappeared the second week of the season with drug problems and never returned. Ron Wolfley, a rookie, showed great promise but couldn't offer the relief a veteran could provide. Stump Mitchell, however, was a bright spot at tailback. A ninth-round draft choice in 1981, he had been a long shot to make the team, but through determination he became one of the toughest backs in the league. Only five-nine, 188 pounds, Stump looks too little to hurt you, but he hits like a freight train and has more determination than Dale Carnegie. He gets my vote for sheer heart, and he came through many times during the season when nobody else cared. The defense spent much of the year playing what we would call a

"Swiss cheese defense"—they were full of holes and they stunk.

So, as we trotted through the shadows of the tunnel and onto the field, Coach Jamieson's attitude meant a lot to me. I was ready. Warm-ups brought a little spark of fire down in my stomach as I whipped pass after pass in a tight spiral and readied for the kickoff. I was going to do it. I couldn't fail, if for no other reason than because I had given Coach Jamieson my word.

Ron Wolfley returned Rafael Septien's opening kickoff to our 26. I turned to listen to one last word of advice from head coach Jim Hanifan, a robust-looking man in his late fifties with a wide face, ruddy complexion, shocking white hair, and an omnipresent cigarette hanging from his lips. Though I respected Hanifan as a head coach, I really wasn't too sure of his abilities. His forte was the offensive line, something he was very adept at, but when it came to the entire scope of the offense I felt he really wasn't aware of what was going on. Furthermore, when the club began suffering, he really lost control of the team. There are few people nicer than Jim, but I was quickly losing respect for his ability to be a leader, something a head coach must be.

"Test the middle, Neil," he rasped, taking a deep drag off his cigarette before releasing a cloud of smoke that trailed away in the wind. I was hardly listening. "Tell those guys up front to get off their butts," he added, louder this time.

I trotted to the back of the huddle and kneeled down, my chin strap dangling, as ten pairs of inquisitive eyes looked back at me. "Here we go," I said, thinking of my first play of the series. Usually, the plays come from the bench, but we generally have a list of predetermined plays, based on down and distance, for me to choose from. "Okay, guys, let's go straight at 'em. Sixty-Power Trap on two." I clapped my hands, snapped my chin strap, and wheeled to face the defense, who stood waiting. Quickly checking the Dallas secondary for any early indications, I sidled up under Randy, whose burly six-three, 270-pound frame was bent over the football. "Blue, seventeeeeeee-six," I yelled. Dallas defensive back Michael Downs began barking commands of his own as the Cowboys' down-linemen began shifting around, a common trait for their "flex" defense. You could sense the nervous tension in the air, a gripping feeling of anticipation evident before the first contact in every game. "Hut . . . hut." The ball slapped into my palms and nearly a ton of beef and muscle surged forward with a clack of pads and grunts as the fans roared in the background. I spun and smoothly slid the ball into the stomach of Stump Mitchell, whose eyes were pressed intensely ahead on a tiny crack of daylight in the line of scrimmage. With a burst of speed, he high-stepped one tackler and got 5 yards before the Cowboys' massive defensive end, John Dutton, brought him down from behind.

On second down, 70-Power Trap got us 3 yards. Things were clicking, and I felt good. On a crucial third and two from our 34-yard-line, I handed off to Stump off the left side, who barely took two steps before colliding headfirst with Randy White. Stump's frame was no match for White's six-five, 280-pound build, and the impact jarred the ball free. It bounced once off the turf and for a split second seemed frozen in space before diving Dallas linebacker Eugene Lockhart made the recovery.

I sure felt bad for Stump, yet I was downright disgusted for the turnover. He's a great athlete whose heart is bigger than his body, and he goes out of his way to help his teammates. Because of his small stature, he never seems to get a fair shot. But he gives 110 percent on special teams and is a magician with the football. His darting, dashing style is similar to a ball on a bumper-pool table—smacking into people, bouncing off, reversing his field, bouncing around, boom, boom, boom, always moving. But his second effort occasionally results in a fumble, which usually is forgivable.

It took Dallas quarterback Danny White just five plays to find Mike Renfro in the end zone for an 18-yard touchdown and a 7-0 lead, and the deafening crowd really started to get on top of us. But my adrenaline was pumping as we came out for our second series, as I was indeed confident we could move the ball against them. In fact, I was playing with a controlled anger. I wanted to win, and every glance at Coach Jamieson reassured my desire. I dropped to throw on first down, and found Tilley on a crossing route for 19 yards. We were rolling, and I was pumped. "Here we go, here we go," I said, my assurance growing by the minute. With Stump slashing for the tough yards on the ground and Pat catching passes with the tenacity of a gritty veteran, we marched 71 yards in eleven plays. On first and goal from the Dallas 2-yard line, Stump slammed over the top to tie the score.

The defense hunkered down and got us the ball back pretty quick. Two plays later, on third and eight from the Cowboys' 45, I blistered Pat's arm with a 41-yard bullet into double coverage; his catch, in traffic, was incredible, but routine for him. My heart was racing. Ron Wolfley dove into the line for a yard, and with second and goal from the Dallas 1, Stump tried to wriggle his way over for the score that would give us the lead. Before I could react, the ball had squirted free. This time Dutton recovered it himself. I unsnapped my helmet with fury and kicked at the turf. Two out of three drives, and we've fumbled twice and scored once. This one game was becoming a summary of the entire season: three steps forward, two steps back. I remembered Chuck Swindoll's book with that title. Moments after the fumble I sat on the bench, my helmet cocked back on my head as I sipped a cup of water. I wasn't going to let this game slip away. *Why does this always happen to us?* I thought, as I outwardly fumed over the situation. I wiped the sweat from my face, wadded up the paper cup, and threw it at the trash can. It went wide right. It was going to be one of those days.

Danny White was having a great afternoon. I really like him. He always looks so intense, so determined, so aware of the situation. You look out there and he's biting his lip, furrowing his brow, giving instructions. He is the essence of a leader. Danny put on a clinic in the second quarter, completing seven-of-nine for 89 yards, including back-to-back touchdowns to Doug Cosbie and Tony Hill. We had countered with a 38-yard field goal by kicker Novo Bojovic, and then a nine-play, 69-yard touchdown drive which left us trailing 21-17. But we moved the ball to the Dallas 46-yard line with 10 seconds left in the first half, and I knew we had time to get some kind of a score.

They were blitzing us to death, sending extra defensive backs after me on every down. Therefore, there weren't enough blockers to protect me; when that happens, somebody's going to get through on every play. But what fans don't always understand is that, as quarterback, it's my responsibility to figure out which guy, and I must communicate to my receivers to take advantage of the absence of that particular defensive back. Then I have to get rid of the ball before they put my lights out. I still get hit, but if I do my job correctly, the pass is completed. If I make my decisions quickly enough and "read" the defense in time, huge gains are possible. So on each play I must determine which player is blitzing, which play best exploits the defense, and which receiver is best for the task.

On this particular play, we wanted Roy Green. Roy is really fast, much faster than Pat, and on this day he appeared healthy. We were pretty sure what defense we would see, and if the cards fell right, we might hit them for a quick score.

The huddle was full of hoarse breathing. Every pant exhaled a ghost of steam that hung suspended in the frigid 34-degree air for several seconds, then vanished. The huge arms of the linemen sparkled with sweat. I looked at the green carpet and noticed the drip, drip, drip of contrasting bright, red blood; someone was bleeding. I stared back into the curious, watery eyes of the offense, sticking my hands under my facemask to quickly warm them with a blast of hot breath.

"Isn't a person in this stadium doesn't know what they're gonna do," I said. "So let's go 847 wide, and be alert for the blitz. Remember the live color is red. Let's catch these guys at their own game."

The anticipation of the 54,125 fans on hand created an ear-splitting roar as I walked to the line of scrimmage, taking a quick glance at the 30-second clock, which was down to 18 seconds and counting. Simultaneously, I noticed the cold stare of strong safety Bill Bates, a vicious defensive back, who was inching nearer and nearer to the line. His fists clinched and opened, clinched and opened; his lips were taut. Going through my mental checklist, I assured myself it was Bates and Everson Walls who were blitzing as I barked the signals.

"Huuuuuuuuut."

I quickly backpedaled, but so did Bates as he retreated into coverage at a furious pace. My heart stopped; Bates wasn't blitzing, and Wells was covering Green! I barely had time to emit a surprised expletive before the hard plastic helmet of Dallas cornerback Dennis Thurman—a speeding cannonball disguised as a football player—found its mark in the small of my back. All the air exploded from my lungs as Thurman ran through the tackle, bending me first backwards, then driving me forward into the turf. My teeth were still jangling when the gun sounded to end the half. I was so angry at myself, I was seething. A quarterback failing to pick up the blitz can be likened to a construction foreman forgetting about a swinging boom headed in his direction. Two or three such errors can really ruin your day—or your career! Coach Jamieson's intense halftime instructions were merely static noise to me as I mentally replayed the first half. Leaning forward in the cool metal chair, I toweled sweat from my face and rubbed my matted, soaking hair. That last play could easily have been a touchdown. Timing is everything. You've got just a few seconds to get the ball off, and it's really a finesse strategy when you're playing against a team that blitzes a lot. And how could I have missed that blitz?

This is what Dallas coaches bank on. They live and die with the idea they're going to get the quarterback before he has a chance to throw. Every time I take that seven-step drop, regardless of whether I get the ball off, I get hit. The Cowboys know that, unless their rhythm is interrupted, late in the game the quarterback is going to be indecisive, unsure, and gun-shy. In other words, they toss him around like a rag doll to the point he fears for his life and loses his ability to make a difference in the outcome.

Unfortunately, the second half started where the first had left off. With 5:23 to play in the third quarter, Danny White went deep down the right sideline and hit Tony Hill in stride for a 53-yard touchdown to up their lead to 28-17. I could feel the game slipping away, but we still had plenty of time. After starting on our 30-yard line, we marched 40 yards in six plays before I hit Pat with a 12-yard pass to get us a first down at the Dallas 18. A quick score here would put us right back in the thick of it.

Seconds before, I had barely overthrown Roy Green in the end zone. Now was the time to try again.

"Roy, you're the man," I said in the huddle. Roy nodded. Turning to the offensive linemen, I rallied for some protection. "Let's all try to get a piece of somebody up there," I told them. "It's getting pretty busy back here."

I took the snap and rolled right, as grunting and heavy footsteps thundered behind me in hot pursuit. I should've stayed in the pocket, but I wanted the big play. The field unfolded before me in a kaleidoscope of red-and-white jerseys. Roy was covered, but out of the corner of my eye, I saw Pat Tilley zipping across the field.

As I began to raise my arm to throw, I was grabbed hard from behind. Big fingers bit into my skin as I was bulldogged like a calf in a rodeo. My legs jerked out from under me, and I slammed headfirst into the turf. Everything went black. My head bounced back viciously, adding whiplash to the concussion administered by the rock-hard turf. The culprit was Jim Jeffcoat, the Cowboys' young and towering defensive end, and he got up and walked away as I lay in a heap on the field.

There's nothing artificial about the pain you get from fake grass, which may be the worst "innovation" ever inflicted on the game of football. That day in Dallas the turf and I had become well acquainted, and my encounter with Jeffcoat cinched the relationship. I rose groggily to my feet, my motor functions intact but my mind unsure of exactly where I was. Hazy-eyed, I approached the bench, but I didn't really recognize all the faces in front of me—I had made it off the field, but had gone to the wrong sideline. Danny White shot me a quizzical look of concern. "Hey man, you okay?" he asked. Thinking I was on the sideline with my teammates, his question sounded pretty stupid to me. "Yeah, I'm fine," I fired back with disgust. "What are you talking about?" Tom Landry reached out for me, but then my head began spinning and I collapsed to one knee, my mind blank and vision blackening. The world was going in and out in swirls of colors, sights, and sounds.

Within seconds, John Omohundro and Jim Shearer, our trainers, were by my side, shoving smelling salts up my nose. This had little effect, though, and I recall them looking at each other as if to say, "Man, he's not even feeling this." For the record, inhaling smelling salts is quite similar to pouring ammonia up your nose; I was sniffing away as if they were roses. They helped me over to the St. Louis sideline and looked at Coach Hanifan blankly. "He's out," John told him.

By this time Scott Brunner, our backup quarterback, had taken over. In seconds, he had been smeared for a 7-yard loss by Mike Hegman and fumbled, with Cowboy linebacker Eugene Lockhart making his second fumble recovery of the day. A few plays later Tony Dorsett scored to push the score to 35-17. We wouldn't score again. Within a 5-minute period we had gone from threatening an upset to being blown out.

Before I knew it, the game was over. My entire body ached. The great hits fans ooh and aah over during the course of a game are translated into masses of purple and blue bruises afterward. I limped to the showers, my half-stumbling gait making me look like I was walking on a bed of nails. I tried to relax as the hot water peppered my skin, but winced when the stream struck the deep blue bruise left by Thurman's hit. A loud ringing tormented my inner ears, and my neck stung sharply with every move.

Some Thanksgiving.

I dressed and called my wife, Laurie, who was back home in St. Louis. Laurie is athletic looking, trim and brisk with beautiful, shoulder-length brown hair and big, brown eyes. We had met after my first NFL season at Portland State, when I was finishing up on my degree. Much more refined and dignified than me, she has a certain class about her which makes her easily likable. Normally very strong-hearted, Laurie was noticeably upset after watching me being thrashed on national television. "Are you okay?" she asked, fighting her emotion. "I'm fine, I'm fine," I said. She hesitated; I knew something else was wrong. "What's going on?" I demanded, unprepared for the answer I would get.

"Your parents called. . . . Your grandmother died."

I leaned my head against the cold locker room wall. My granny, Sigred Lomax, a humble woman whose smile brought joy into everyone's life, was one of my sweetest memories. The news hit me harder than the Cowboy blitz. Just two months earlier I had flown home for my grandfather's funeral; when Ralph passed away there was an immediate emotional letdown for Grandma. Now, on Thanksgiving, whatever fight she'd had left had ebbed away. A resident in a Portland nursing home, she had been given her turkey dinner and was watching our game on television. When an attendant checked her later, she had died.

The flight home to St. Louis seemed to take forever. I stared out the window into the blackness, the drone of the jet engines drawing my thoughts away. My head throbbed. The thought of my grandmother brought tears to my eyes. For all the good things that go along with being an NFL quarterback, there are times when the much-publicized "invincibility" that supposedly goes hand-in-hand with my job is strangely absent. Alone on a plane full of people, I sensed a closeness to God; my mind recalled what a youth pastor had taught me ten years before. "When all your strength is used up, when you've got nothing left, you have to have an inner strength deeper than your own," he had said. Fortunately, I heeded his advice. In my bruised and beaten state, I was more thankful than ever for the love and faith reciprocated in my relationship with Jesus Christ. When the coaches don't care anymore, when the fans don't seek my autograph, when the big paychecks run out, God will always be there, sticking closer than a brother.

Leaning back on the headrest, I forced a half-smile. When I come up on the short end of life's stick, it's nice to know I have something stronger to rely on than the glamour of being an NFL quarterback. Because sometimes the glamour hurts.

I closed my eyes and fell asleep.

2

The "Ghetto" of Lake Oswego

"The child sees everything which has to be experienced and learned as a doorway. So does the adult. But what to the child is an entrance is to the adult only a passage."

—Nietzsche

My hands were sweating as I stepped to the plate to face Cincinnati Reds pitcher Pedro Ramos in the bottom of the twelfth inning with the bases loaded. It was mid-September 1969, and my Dodger teammates and I were in a showdown for first place in the National League West. The handle of the bat was slippery as I took a few practice cuts. The crowd roared as I dug in with my left foot and cocked the bat behind my right shoulder. Meanwhile, Vince Scully, the voice of the Los Angeles Dodgers, was thrilling his listeners with unparalleled commentary.

"Lo-max, the Dodgers' big gun throughout this in-credi-ble series, is in a staredown now with big Pedro Ramos, the tough lefthander."

Ramos took a long look before starting his windup. I licked my lips nervously. Ramos made his delivery: a fastball right down the middle. I was surprised he'd try to fool a veteran like me with a pitch like that. With apologies to Dodger first baseman Wes Parker, for whom I was pinch-hitting, I stepped forward and leaned into the pitch, feeling an almost spiritual purge as the bat made solid contact with the ball.

"Oh my, Lo-max really got into that one," roared an excited Scully. "What a shot. It's a deep drive down the left field line . . . way back, way back . . . it hits the inside of the foul pole for a game-winning hit. The stunned Pedro Ramos looks on in bewilderment as the big kid from Lake Oswego, Oregon, rounds the bases! The Dodgers win it!"

In the best form a ten-year-old could muster, I trotted around the bases, being careful to touch each one—the bush, the dirt spot, the tree, and finally, home plate, a piece of cardboard. My imagination was in overdrive as Dodgers pitcher Bill Singer rushed from the dugout to hug me. My Los Angeles teammates poured in around me, slapping my back and shouting with enthusiasm.

"The Los Angeles Dodgers," lauded Scully. "In one of the wildest pennant races to date, the Dodgers take first in the West, in front of San Francisco and Atlanta." I hung around for hours after the game doing interviews with NBC and never grew tired of the hundreds of fans who besieged me for autographs.

Long before I ever entertained crowds as quarterback of the St. Louis Cardinals, I performed—brilliantly—before countless millions of imaginary fans in the backyard of our Lake Oswego home. During my boyhood days I imagined I was a star in the major leagues, the NBA, the NFL, and even the PGA tour, depending on the time of year. Never thrilled about playing before empty seats, I was compelled to also fill in the background noise of screaming, stomping, yelling fans. The din would be occasionally interrupted for expert commentary from either Vince Scully or Howard Cosell, neither of whom ever criticized my play. Instead, it was always my game-saving, diving catch of a line drive down third base, or my last-second, 65-yard bomb for a touchdown, or my chip-in for an eagle that caught their attention. If only announcers were so kind today—there's a big difference between fantasy and reality.

Located eight miles southwest of the city of Portland on the Willamette River, Lake Oswego is a great place to live and where I still call home. Great fir trees point skyward in every direction, and lakes are plentiful. The view to the east features snowcapped Mount Hood, which is about fifty miles away in the Cascade Range. A three-mile-long lake, the area's namesake, lies directly in the heart of the city of 22,751.

During the first few decades of the century, the wealthy used the lake for summer residences and expensive development of lakeside property. Thereafter, it became a year-round residential community. The city of Oswego was incorporated in 1910, but was changed to Lake Oswego in 1959 with the incorporation of Lake Grove. Many of Portland's wealthier citizens have made Lake Oswego home, which often casts the impression that only the rich live there.

Carmen Drive, where my two brothers, my sister, and I grew up, however, was a lower middle-class residential section of what used to be Lake Grove, which we called "the groove" or "the ghetto" of Lake Oswego. My parents, David and Carol, remind me of the quaint one-story home in which we were reared, and where they still live: very humble and unassuming, but radiating the warmth of a crackling fireplace.

The pleasant tone and easy smile of my dad, a music teacher, has made him a favorite of Portland High School students for more than thirty years. Never caring to color coordinate his socks,

Dad always opts for his trademark white tube socks, which clearly are given more to comfort than style, much like the spongy shocks of a slow-moving luxury automobile.

Mom is a healthy contrast to Dad, both in temperament and personality. Grittier than sandpaper and with determination stronger than garlic, she has deep, thoughtful eyes which always appear to be looking through you, as opposed to at you. The supreme air of confidence she developed through scores of AAU swimming victories as a teenager was evident during my childhood, and much of it rubbed off—today self-confidence is a common trait of most every Lomax offspring. A schoolteacher herself for some time, Mom understood kids; she ran a loose ship around the house, but she was one tough cookie if her wrath was incurred.

Together, they harbor such pride in their children they feel a physical part of every plateau of success or valley of disappointment we experience.

I always held my older brother, Mitch, in high regard, perhaps because he was the only person capable of beating me in sports in my early years. Tall and lanky with darker hair than the rest of us, Mitch was a guiding force in my life. Terry, two years my junior, faced a no-win situation daily with the overpowering confidence of his older brothers; like a scrappy gunfighter who blazes away gamely but always finds himself one bullet short. His interests turned to fine arts and theater. Valorie, the baby of the family and five years younger than me, has blossomed into an assertive, independent young lady, but was much the opposite in her childhood, maybe because she didn't feel like jockeying for attention in the midst of three boisterous boys.

Playful laughter at our house was interrupted often by horrible arguments among us boys. From day one, I was a fierce competitor, and unable to conquer Mitch as a child, I turned on Terry to release my feelings. In sports, I owned Terry, but occasionally he would manipulate me into a drawing contest or a clay-modeling contest, which was his forte. Once, when I was eight (Terry was six), we worked on building clay fortresses for several hours. I had made only a few crude clay men when I noticed Terry had an elaborate network of castles, guns, and soldiers. I couldn't believe it. Refusing to accept defeat, I announced, "That's pretty nice, Terry, but, oh no, here comes a rock storm." I began dropping rocks from every angle, smashing his handiwork into oblivion as he tearfully screamed at me to stop. I was heartless and never considered how I might be hurting him emotionally.

The backyard was in a constant frenzy of activity. Dad, whose hands were an extension of his mechanical prowess, built facsimiles of tanks and planes in which we constantly wormed around, the "ack-ack-ack-ack" of make-believe machine guns blazing and furious games of Kick the Can were also another favorite. Valorie often would sit idly by, as she was not permitted to participate because we never deemed her old enough. When she was six and we were nine, eleven, and thirteen, we would tell her, "When you're nine, you can play Kick the Can." Of course, by the time she was nine, we had upped the age to twelve. But I was very protective of Val and remember many times when Mom and Dad would be out at night playing bridge and I, at age six or seven, would tuck her in and read her a story and stroke her sandy brown hair until she went to sleep.

Imaginary games in the backyard often included one or both of my brothers, but Mitch represented a real problem. If either Mitch or I lost, it meant a fight, and virtually every matchup with him led to Howard Cosell describing another colorful clash: "Oh no, laaadies and gentlemen . . . a fight has bro-ken out on the play-ing field." So Terry was my favorite opponent, because Terry might get angry about his defeat but he seldom had the guts to fight me. My extreme feeling of superiority meant I could never lose, even if I had to change the rules, and Terry's complete frustration often took the form of outrage.

Our one-on-one football games were classics, however, and contained all the drama of the real thing. While I was the fans, the commentator, and, of course, the home team, I would make Terry be the Colts or the Oilers or another long-shot underdog. The bedroom we shared became my locker room, while Terry's clubhouse was actually my sister's room across the hall. After imaginary referees would give the announcement of "five minutes to kickoff," we'd trot down the "tunnel," out the back door, and onto the playing field.

Meanwhile, my nonstop commentary would be updating fans on every aspect of the matchup, including the weather, vital statistics, and naturally, how "un-stopp-able" these awesome Packers were with Neil Lomax at quarterback. Since I controlled the television networks (which would get me a lawsuit today), Terry seldom was given any air time, which always infuriated him. About that time, I would get my fill. "OH NO," I'd yell, "A FIGHT HAS BROKEN OUT IN THE TUNNEL BETWEEN THE TWO TEAMS." I would pummel Terry, then interview him; he would scream with adolescent fury and vow to kill me and the Packers.

Dust hung in the air over the backyard one afternoon after one of the hardest-fought battles ever between the Colts and the Packers. Sweat ran down our little faces and our clothes were streaked with dirt as the game wound down. Terry's sheer determination had kept it close, and he was trailing by three, with only minutes to play. This particular knock-down-and-drag-out had even attracted Mitch and several of his friends as spectators, and my reputation as football king was riding on the outcome. Terry, who had possession, recognized his chance at an upset victory, and little by little drove down the field. On the last play of the game, Terry hurtled over the goal line for the winning touchdown. "I won, I won," Terry exclaimed, as his imaginary Baltimore Colts teammates mobbed him at mid-field. He was in ecstasy; I was providing "the viewers at home" with as many details as possible.

"Incredible," I announced. "It appears as if the Colts have upset the mighty Packers. Wait, the referees are circled together at the goal line. Oh noooooo," I chortled. "There's a flag on the play. They're bringing it all the way back and tacking on a 15-yard penalty."

A line of tears streaked Terry's dirty face. Despite a valiant effort on the final play, he failed to score. Sobbing in frustration, he stayed on the ground, his head in his hands. My teammates carried me off the field. To the victor go the spoils, right?

*   *   *

My cocky, outgoing personality made me a highly visible kid as early as grade school, where I discovered self-assuredness worked not only on Terry, but also on my peers. My first pair of leather, low-top Adidas sneakers coincided with my sixth-grade year, and I was Big Boy on Campus as I strutted down the sidewalk, making it clear to others that, "Hey, man, these shoes are sooo expensive."

Pat Mendenhall, a mischievous, short, rascally kid, was my bopping-around buddy. Pat, now a Houston stockbroker, lived catty-corner to me, and we were inseparable as kids. My first and last political aspirations took place the same year, as I ran for student body president with Pat as my campaign manager. I made lavish promises during my unabashed speeches and vowed to uphold my slogan, "If you want a good deal, vote for Neil." I won easily, and the victory helped to further build my self-confidence.

My parents say they remember those times as a breeding ground for the sense of command that eventually would become a force on the football field. Already, I was proving unstoppable on the fifth- and sixth-grade teams. Tall for my age, I cut through small grade school kids like John Madden busting through paper walls.

I can't recall the exact day when the blackboard began to get fuzzy from my perch in the back of the classroom that year, but I vividly remember the eye checkup at the doctor's office. When the doctor told me I was nearsighted, I gasped. Glasses, at that age, were a fate worse than death—the biggest crisis I had ever faced. Athletes, my gosh, they never wore glasses, so I seldom wore mine. The adjustment would take years, and Mrs. Dutton's math class in the sixth grade sure didn't help matters. Cool guys sat in the back of the room, but from that vantage point I couldn't see the blackboard. Not to be outdone, I would arrive early and copy all the problems from the board, then move to the back of the room. This worked fine, until the day she walked in, lectured for a while, then erased some of the problems and scribbled up new ones. Turning to the class, she rested her eyes on me. Praying she wouldn't say my name, I melted into my seat. "Neil," she said, oblivious to the cold sweat breaking out on my body, "give us an answer for this one." Refusing the prodding of my conscience to put my glasses on, I stood up and squinted for all I was worth. Suddenly, Eric Mailen, sitting to my left, intervened. "Mrs. Dutton," he said, "from back here, the way the sunlight's hitting the board, you can't see." Phew. Talk about saving face. For a sixth grader, that's a serious crisis. I accepted my fate by junior high, though, when I began wearing my glasses regularly. Today I usually wear contacts, although I've grown to like my glasses over the years.

It was early in my first year of junior high school and the basketball courts were packed. Time and again my eyes were drawn to the same spunky, short kid whose mouth was as fast as his shot, which wasn't bad. Brown-haired and meticulous, he was more elusive than a collar button, his quick feet moving like a pack of rabbits. I was instantly attracted to him. Over the next few months, Stuart Gaussoin and I became the best of friends; Batman and Robin, Jonathan and David, Damon and Pythias, all rolled into one. Whenever the action got a little too furious for Stu, I would jump to his side in his defense. What he lacked in size he made up for in fearlessness. Together, we went virtually unchallenged.

Always concerned about my grades, I would do anything if I thought for a minute it could help me get ahead. Which was why, in the eighth grade, I volunteered to play the tuba; the teacher enticed aspiring tuba players with an automatic A in the course. Knowing I had the grade in the bag, I spent my entire tuba tenure horsing around. Our band teacher, Steve Richey, grew to regret ever putting a tuba in my hands. Talking loudly through the tuba was like having a portable public address system, and during band practice, I would deafen the flute players in

front of me with startling, out-of-nowhere blasts. Practice would
be in full swing, with everyone listening intently to Mr. Richey's
instructions, when I would discreetly raise my tuba to my lips.
"HOW ARE YOU GUYS DOING DOWN THERE?" I'd
roar. Kids literally jumped off their seats and music flew in the air
as I laughed hysterically.

"Hey, up there," a red-faced Mr. Richey would yell. "NO tuba
talking. Knock it off."

Athletically, it seemed I was always one step ahead of Stu,
though in high school we both shared the spotlight. In the ninth
grade, I made the A team, and Stu made the B team, but by our
sophomore year, there was no question we were going to be quite
a tandem for the Lake Oswego Lakers. Stuart had blazing speed
for a high school kid, and he returned punts, ran with bruising au-
thority, and made circus catches look easy. He had a gift for
catching the football and proved it at every opportunity. The difference in our upbringings—mine rather poor, his, middle-
class—made our relationship that much more unique. But sometimes, even though I knew Stu didn't look down on me, I was
embarrassed at the lack of extra money in my family. Many times
my brothers, Val, and I would be the only ones on the school bus;
with the kind of money in Lake Oswego, most kids had their own
cars to drive to school.

Meanwhile, I began blossoming as a stable, confident leader
under center. After I spent a solid year on the junior varsity team,
I was excited about the upcoming year. Early in the fall of 1975, I
returned home from school and barely had time to set my books
down before my mother practically accosted me with that week's
Lake Oswego Review. "Neil, listen to this," she said, pointing to
an article in the sports section. ". . . as much of a candidate for
the starting quarterback position is Neil Lomax. Lomax, a junior
up from the JV team, is the Lakers' alter ego at the quarterback
slot. He is proficient at passing. He has the sight to see . . . the
arm to throw." Excitedly, she grabbed a pair of scissors and
clipped the story, carefully placing it with some other family
memorabilia. Eventually, this became a sore spot for me, when
clipping newspapers and magazines became my parents' hobby.

Boyd Crawford, our high school coach, was instrumental in my development as both a player and person, and today, he's still at Lake Oswego molding lives and men. Recognizing me as a leader with "workable" skills, he felt I had the raw talent necessary. My progress directly mirrored his input. He had solid morals and values and asked the same of his players. A hard, disciplined worker, he asked us to give 110 percent all the time. Kneeling with his team on cold locker room floors before many Friday night high school battles, he would challenge us as men. "Winning," he would say, "is a by-product of preparation . . . and nobody is better prepared than we are." Even now, I realize there still is no substitute for preparation. Coach Crawford was a role model for me, and I will always be thankful to him for setting the foundation of my career.

But no amount of preparation on the football field could ready me for what Mitch was beginning to experience in his life during this time. Because of the independent, leader-type image I was rapidly becoming known for, I was never a typical "little brother" to Mitch. He resented me so that whenever I'd ride with him to the golf course, he'd make me ride in the backseat; I'd play the back nine while he played the front nine to keep from being seen with me.

All of us kids were very self-centered and prideful; therefore, when Mitch began to change, we took notice. Mitch would burst in from a Young Life meeting, and it was all he could do to contain his excitement. "Hey, Neil," he'd say breathlessly. "It was cool. They play the guitar, sing fast music you can clap to, and really have fun. It's not like church at all. And there's even good-looking girls." I'd pretend not to care, though inside I was dying of curiosity. Mitch began spending more and more time with a Young Life counselor named Brian Boucher—playing basketball, shooting pool, always something.

In the summer of 1973, around the same time as the Richard Nixon Watergate scandal, Mitch took off with a Young Life contingent to Camp Malibu. The camp, a reclusive Christian hideaway in Vancouver, Canada, requires two-day passage by boat to get there. There, Mitch accepted Jesus Christ as his Savior, and when he came home, the change was like night and day. Mitch decided to support our parents, right or wrong, and became consumed with sharing with the entire family what God had done in his life. The tension between my parents was getting unsettling, and the addition of "religion" magnified the problems. And until Mitch's self-imposed change, there was absolutely no spiritual direction in our home, because we never really went to church as a family. His whole attitude toward me changed without me really doing anything. He began to love me, which blew me away. I couldn't believe it.

Once he caught me stealing change out of his drawer. "What are you doing?" he asked. "Nothing," I stammered. I was so embarrassed, but Mitch didn't say another word. He just smiled. His loving actions spoke louder than words after his conversion; it was evident he was a different person. As for stealing, I never took another thing that belonged to somebody else, and I'm still ashamed when I think about that incident. But for some time I remained wary of Mitch, even cold. He would offer his help or attention, and I would mock him. "Hey, reverend," I'd needle. He'd only smile with forgiveness.

Mitch's life was the only Bible our family ever read for the next several years. Prior to my junior year, almost two years after Mitch's conversion, I decided to see for myself. The stories I'd been hearing about the Young Life meetings—about Jesus and miracles and all kinds of crazy stuff like that—were fine and dandy, but I kept thinking, *Why does everybody have this genuine feeling of love, and I don't?* I couldn't figure out what was missing. I didn't have drinking problems or a drug habit. I had friends. I was the starting pitcher of the baseball team and going to be the starting quarterback of the football team. I didn't need a crutch. But still my life somehow seemed empty.

After a long talk with Stu ("C'mon Stu, we'll have a good time . . . there's girls there"), I convinced him to go to a Young Life camp. In preparation for the long road trip to Malibu, Canada, we smuggled a fifth of Vodka in an overnight bag. As it turned out, I discovered a different kind of "high"—an everlasting one.

When we finally got there, it was a classic case of, "Wow, this place is incredible." I thought they'd taken us to heaven. No streets, no roads, just God's beauty everywhere. Snowcapped mountains were visible in every direction, and the lakes reflected a still image of the cloudless blue skies splashed with sunshine. They had games of every kind, and I quickly asserted myself in golf, watermelon-seed spitting, obstacle course, and other contests which I won handily. During the evenings they held assemblies, and various speakers would reiterate over and over the wonderful things God had done; the same stuff I'd been hearing for months back home. Finally, the true message began piercing my prideful heart: "Man, you need to make a decision about a personal relationship with Jesus Christ." The last night of the camp, I walked out of the assembly.

The silence was deafening as I wandered off alone. Trees swayed in the wind, their images outlined against a moonlit sky. The occasional rumbling of a crashing wave against the shore would interrupt the stillness. I panned the skies and was awed by the number of stars dotting the black backdrop.

Suddenly, I felt close to God. My self-confidence, though, was strangely absent. I needed Christ, and I could feel it. It was as if I had cut through all the paperwork and now was dealing directly with Him. "Lord," I said softly, "I know You're out there. Hey, I know I'm a sinner. I know I've been hearing about a better way but I failed to do anything, and I'm still empty inside. But I want You to come into my life and now, at this time, take over my life. That's all, Lord. Thanks." I glanced around and waited for something spectacular to happen, like fireworks or a miracle or a clear complexion. Anything. Nothing did. But I knew I was changed.

After having known Christ for barely more than a few hours, I sensed He was going to have an impact on my life. I realized that our entire family had been wallowing in the routine of life: get up, do your thing, go to bed, start over. Jesus was exciting, fresh, *alive*, and I had a strong sense things were going to change for the better.

That night in bed, I thought about how it would be to share my new beliefs back in school. It wouldn't be easy. Portland was a far cry from Los Angeles or New York, but by the mid-seventies the "love culture" had caught up with us. All the guys knew certain girls who were "catchable," as well as where and how to get beer or pot. Though I noticed the girls, the pot and alcohol had never really interested me. But "having a good time" was the basis of many friendships. Somehow I would have to show my friends that knowing Christ could be fun.

On the long boat trip back to Seattle, from where we bused home, I discovered that Stuart, too, had accepted Christ during the camp. We spent the whole trip telling each other, "Together, we can change Lake Oswego High School." We wanted to be leaders, be radicals for Christ, so we began to take an active part in youth classes at Mountain Park Church. There, youth pastor Ron Kincaid started urging us to "press toward the mark."

Ron, who is now my pastor at Sunset Presbyterian in Portland and still a close friend, was responsible for much of my spiritual growth. An agile, athletic man of medium height with brown hair and eyes, Ron is soft-spoken, articulate, and has innate shepherding abilities. In August of 1975 I began attending his weekly youth meetings. Every week he approached our group with three questions: 1. How are you doing in your relationship with God? 2. How are you doing in your relationship with family, friends, or other people? and 3. How are you reaching out to somebody who doesn't know Christ? Those questions became a hallmark of our times together, and we held one another responsible in those areas. The growth of our youth group, which we called the Salt Company (as in "salt" of the earth), paralleled the growing popularity Stu and I were feeling as high school football stars. Our impact on the group was necessary, according to Ron, who would tell us, "I'm looking to you guys for leadership."

Stu and I responded. When the group began, we had ten to fifteen members. By our senior year, there were more than one hundred in attendance each week. And the lessons Ron spoke of are still etched in my mind. "Keep the Lord first, and He will give you all that you need in life," he used to tell us. "If you put your focus on just football, or women, or money, or fame, that's all you're going to get." Psalms 37:4, 5 was one of his favorite texts, and I can still hear him pleading with us as youths to "keep the Lord first, and He will give you the desires of your heart."

The year 1975 was earmarked by a period of national unrest. All the energy that had been pumped into the Vietnam War controversy had yet to be redirected. President Richard M. Nixon had resigned over the Watergate scandal, which had also run several more high-ranking officials out of Washington. FBI agents captured Patty Hearst, an heir in the publishing clan, after she was kidnapped and then had joined forces with her abductors in several bank robberies.

It was amidst all this national turmoil that Mitch headed off to college. The whole country seemed to be seeking a direction for itself, and my personal problems seemed pretty small in the scope of current events. But Mitch had been the Rock of Gibraltar in my life, and his sudden absence cast a tumultuous feeling over me. My relationship with God in the past year or so had been shaken a few times, but I never drifted too far away. Stu, however, found it quite easy to blend with the world, and though he insisted he really wanted to be different, his bouncing back and forth frustrated me. Now, without Mitch to lean on, I was faced with having to serve Christ alone. It was time for me to pull up anchor on my spiritual boat and cast out to sea, and I was reluctant. Mitch hadn't been gone any time, though, when I scribbled off a note to him:

Mitch,

I hope you are having the best time of your life up there. I know I did. Things are okay down here, but the weather is pretty shabby (rain). Today is Dad's birthday, and we went to see the Timbers play St. Louis for the semifinals game. A record crowd of 33,567 witnessed a brutal contest with the Timbers coming out on top 1-0.

The Timbers already beat Seattle again 2-1 in OT to go on to the semifinals.

Getting away from the jock talk . . . Stu and I had a good trip coming back from Vancouver. Jesus Christ is giving me a little bit of trouble. It's hard to be patient, but believe me, I'm still there, though, and the Bible is helping me out. Stu doesn't really know it but he's two-facing himself. Hopefully when you get back you can help me and Stu to get back on Christ's path for eternity. Christ is still my Main Man and I'm going to need Him, especially through the daily doubles and the 1975 football season. I pray for Mom, Dad, Val, and Terry and for you. I hope it will all work out with Jesus Christ's help. I'm trying to obey and consume the fruits of God, and it's bringing me some relief, even though friends cause temptations. I know He will lead me in the right direction for eternity. He is Lord, and my belief in Him will bring me security and happiness.

In Our Lord's Name, Love Between Brothers,
Neil

But despite the impact of my brother and Ron's messages, there were several times when I refused to use my Christian judgment and insisted on learning the hard way. Sometimes teenagers just can't be told; they must experience a painful lesson. The tension involved in being a Christian teenager is incredible; there's always a host of kids trying to entice you into doing something wrong. Rationalizing a situation, such as "one little drink won't hurt," only complicates the situation, when you should just walk away. In the midst of a great baseball season (and a .400 batting average) my junior year, I attended the spring dance with my girl friend, Maria Badgley, who today stars in the ABC-TV soap opera "Loving." We pulled into the parking lot, and all the senior guys were standing around with their girl friends. "Hey," they yelled, "we're having a little toast. Why don't you join us?" In an effort to fit in, I rationalized the situation. *How can a little champagne hurt?* I reasoned, taking a glass from them. Glass after glass went down the chute, and being a novice drinker, I was staggering in no time. Like Chevy Chase turned loose in a china shop, I was instantly the life of the event—dancing, swinging, joking, and hassling the faculty, to the delight of my friends. Time and sobriety were elapsing quickly, and my alcohol-saturated brain became foggier by the minute.

About an hour into the dance I lost touch with reality, and, from that point, there are conflicting reports of my actions. I honestly don't remember entirely. According to reliable sources, I took Maria home—miraculously—between vomiting spasms. Upon reaching my house, I zoomed back and forth, in and out of the driveway, before being rescued by my dad, who retrieved the car and put me to bed. The school called my parents and informed them of my outrageous behavior. This resulted in my first and last suspension from participating in a sport: I was banned from the baseball team for a week.

My confession to Coach Pat Byrne led to a lenient sentence, but that week seemed like an eternity. Obviously, I felt I had let down my parents, teachers, peers, and Ron Kincaid. The fact that people looked up to me as a Christian made the situation particularly embarrassing, but it was important for me to learn that faith alone doesn't keep you from making mistakes. Fortunately, I can look back and laugh about that night and count it as a learning experience. But I'm thankful God was looking out for me, because each year there are thousands of teenagers who never make it home. All of God's plans for my life could have been lost in the smoldering, crumpled steel of a fatal car accident, simply because of one poor decision.

Stuart's flair for independence, combined with my cockiness and ego, presented problems for both of us. Stuart's parents had given him a car at sixteen, and we were super cool tooling around school in his wheels. His parents, Roy and Shirley Gaussoin, were an upper-middle class couple who tried to please him, but his demanding demeanor always made them feel as if they had fallen short. His parents could be strict when they chose to be, but he took them for granted. Constantly pampered, he would occasionally test others' limits to see how much he could get by with. We'd double date, and his mother would tell him, "Stuart, call us at 10:00 P.M. sharp." Just to test her fortitude, he'd call at 10:05, and she would ground him. It was a constant struggle, both physically and spiritually.

Nevertheless, we persisted at being Christians, and Ron's tenacity had a lot to do with it. "People with money and success feel they can do anything they want," he would say. "Accountability is important. Learn to be accountable to God now, and when He knows you can be trusted, He will bless you." Boldness was Ron's forte; never did he pass up an opportunity to ask us big, tough high school football players if we were "spending time in the Bible, still getting to church on Sunday . . . or are you trying to be a Lone Ranger Christian?"

Stu and I developed such an intensity for Christ that we never hesitated to give God the glory for whatever circumstances we were facing. After a big 27-14 victory over Reynolds High School on October 9, 1976, Stuart, who had recovered a clutch fumble and returned a punt for a touchdown, nearly held a camp revival in the locker room. "We play for God," he told a reporter with the *Oregonian*. Sweat dripping from his matted hair, mud covering him from head to toe, Stuart continued: "We don't get much recognition, but we have a great team, a great coach in Boyd Crawford, and a great God."

Such quotes became common in the Lake Oswego locker room, and one writer even mentioned that our club had a "unique outspokenness in regard to religion and faith." And we believed it made a difference in the way we played. Whether it did or not, it made a difference in our lives.

Winning helped, of course. A month after the win over Reynolds, on November 5, we faced our crosstown rival, Lakeridge High, for the Wilco League Championship. Running the option, I took the third snap of the game and bounced outside, spun away from the grasp of a defensive lineman, ran over a defensive back, and, with the crowd tearing the place apart, continued down the sideline for a 63-yard touchdown. What a thrill! That set the tone for the game, and we won 24-17.

Ron missed the game, but his prayers had been with us. Less than a week later, I got this note:

Neil:

I'm sorry I missed your game. You really had a fine game that night. Keep up your good attitude of playing for Christ. I cherish your friendship.

Love,
Ron Kincaid

Through Ron's shepherding, Stuart and I stayed in the Word during our senior year, preparing ourselves for life after high school. I continued to stay in touch with Mitch and fired this letter off to him on November 19, 1976:

Mitch,

Well, how's college life treating you? I really hope that Jesus Christ is always with you and helping you through this semester. I experienced His love tremendously through the football season, and I don't think I could've had the confidence unless I knew He was present in my life. It was a great season.

I got a job (as a messenger) replacing Ted Allen at the Community Bank in Lake Oswego. I get $2.25 an hour, and it's great driving around in that car.

Hey, I've been really praying for you and that you're doing okay and living the life-style that Jesus wants you to. We all miss you here, especially me. I have really misunderstood you, but since you left for college I have found the responsibility of growing up hard. Also, how much I love you as my Christian brother. You have really changed in every standpoint of your life. Your Christian love for others is super.

Write back soon.

Your Christian Brother in Jesus' Name,
Neil

Although I had completed 65 percent of my passes as a senior at an obscure high school, I knew my chances of playing college football were slim-to-none. Darrell "Mouse" Davis, then head coach at Portland State, who thoroughly scouted the area high schools himself for local talent, later admitted I threw so seldom that "if you wanted to see Neil throw, you had to get there for warmups." In fact, I had placed more hope on a baseball scholarship.

Christmas was only weeks away. I was in good spirits as I lay on my bed reading *Sports Illustrated* one evening. My dad rapped on the door, entered, and sat down alongside me. His gentle eyes burned underneath his furrowed brow, making it obvious that something was on his mind. "Son," he said, emitting a long sigh, "we really don't have the money to send you to college without help from somewhere. I'm sorry." Instantly, he had my attention. College was something I'd thought seriously about, but wondered where my "big chance" would come from. Dad didn't cry, but his eyes were red. Dad seemed more hurt by the news than I was, and I was embarrassed for him. He was doing all he could on his schoolteacher's income, and he was terribly frustrated. "We're really hoping you have a good year in baseball. If you have a good year in baseball," he continued, "who knows what will happen."

Not a single offer had come in from football, but I was fully expecting a great senior year in baseball.

My high hopes were due to the success of my junior year. Jack Dunn, baseball coach at Portland State, had offered me a position on his team, but, unfortunately, made no mention of financial help. Letters from small NAIA colleges were popping up in our mailbox, but each school basically presented little more than a "pay to play" situation for either my football or baseball skills. It made even less sense to travel across the country and still have to pay for an education. Mitch was attending Oregon State, and after several visits with him and his "frat rats," I had almost resigned myself to giving my senior baseball season my best shot, then finding a way to attend OSU as a nonathlete.

February was almost over, and a dreary rain was pelting the streets as I walked home from school one afternoon. My mind was on the Portland Trailblazers, who, despite not winning their division, were dominating in the National Basketball Association play-offs and had a good shot at making the finals. The door slammed behind me as I went over to the table and took off my coat, which dripped water onto the floor. There on the counter was an envelope with my name on it. The proud, green Viking symbol of Portland State was in the upper lefthand corner. *Jack Dunn might've come across with a little money after all,* I thought, momentarily imagining myself in a Portland State baseball uniform as I tore the letter open. My expression changed to shock when I read the contents:

Dear Neil:

The purpose of this letter is to notify you of our offer of an athletic grant at Portland State University. This athletic grant consists of tuition and $50 per term.

Sincerely,
Mouse Davis
Head Football Coach
Portland State University

3

The Big Cheese

"Mouse Davis offers a new concept to football, something it desperately needs. Many NFL teams have asked me how this offense can be stopped. Well, if you have a guy under center with talent and a quick gun, it's all over. You can't stop it."

—Don Klosterman,
former NFL general manager

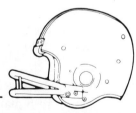

It was a rare cloudless March afternoon in 1977. I anxiously pulled the car into the parking lot of Civic Stadium, taking time out of my after-school job as a messenger boy for a local bank to get a glimpse of Portland State's spring practice. The wind was chilly but the sun was bright, and I shaded my eyes as I walked through the tunnels and onto the outskirts of the football field.

The Portland State Vikings were running through a brisk practice routine. In the middle of hulking, helmeted warriors stood a short, pudgy man wearing shorts and a Portland State Football T-shirt, hands on knees, whistle hanging from his neck. Mouse Davis. I'd read about him in the local papers, and his larger-than-life reputation sparked my curiosity. Occasionally he'd grab his baseball hat and work over a wad of chewing gum any sixth grader would envy, a sure sign that he was deep in thought. "Itty, itty bitty guys," he yelled in a deep, guttural baritone. The man was constant activity, be it mental or physical. "Let's do it right. Move, move move. Get your buttskis in geeeear!"

But it was the motion of the players that really held my attention. Wide receivers were swirling out of everywhere. Some ran deep, some turned up, some ran across the field. Lines of receivers and quarterbacks were perpetually moving in opposite directions in a perfectly timed, machinelike operation.

"Huuuuuut." The quarterback dropped back, kind of rolling to his right or left. Pads clacked. Receivers scrambled in every direction.

"Atta baby, atta baby," Davis encouraged, watching every movement of his troops. A receiver shuffle-stepped and broke inside 40 yards away. Without hesitation, the quarterback laid it up. The receiver never broke stride as he made the catch. I was certainly impressed. A shrill whistle split the air. Apparently, Davis wasn't.

"No, babe," he told the quarterback in a firm but forgiving voice. "Like this." Patiently, in slow motion, he reenacted the steps of the quarterback, exaggerating each precise movement. The quarterback nodded. Another blast of Davis's whistle and eleven fresh players were lined up and ready to go. It was the fastest-moving practice I'd ever witnessed. The Mouse Davis system was carefully outlined in his mind. Even today, others try to imitate it, some understand it, but no one grasps it like him. It's his baby. The Run 'n' Shoot, he called it.

"Phew," I muttered, a grin spreading on my face. At Lake Oswego High School we seldom threw the ball, much less on almost every play. I shook my head.

*   *   *

Darrell was the fifth and final child born to the Davises in the small, farming community of Palouse, Washington, in 1934. "I always told 'em the best came last," he would say whenever recounting his childhood. The family moved to Hermiston, Oregon, when he was in the second grade, then to Portland during his fifth-grade year. Although a fine athlete, his height and small hands always presented problems. Playing second base in one of his first high school baseball games as a freshman, a throw came in hard and he dropped the ball. "Nice catch, Mouse," joked his oldest brother Don, a senior outfielder, in reference to his kid brother's tiny hands. The name stuck. By his senior year, even the teachers didn't know his real name.

As an eighth grader, Mouse decided he wanted to be a football coach, namely because, "I had it figured out by then I was never gonna grow big enough to be a pro athlete." His theory was there are two ways to professional football: playing or coaching. "Even in my high school yearbook, my goal was to be head coach. That basically says that at a young, tender age I was relatively screwed up already."

His little hands served him well, however, as the starting quarterback at the Oregon College of Education, where he led his team to three straight championships from 1952 through 1954. A true student of the game, Mouse wasn't always the best athlete on the field, but "I was always the best prepared. At least I knew what I was supposed to do, even if I physically wasn't capable." His inquisitive thinking laid the groundwork for his life's work, which took on a unique twist.

The actual Run 'n' Shoot offense was conceived in 1958, when Glenn (Tiger) Ellison, a high school coach in Middletown, Ohio, first posted two wide receivers on each sideline and two slotbacks just outside each tackle. One slotback went in motion on nearly every play, lessening the defense's ability to disguise coverages. The formation overloaded three receivers on one side of the field, with each receiver able to "convert" to seven possible routes on every play.

In 1965, as the freshman coach at Ohio State University under Woody Hayes, Ellison wrote the first version of *Run and Shoot: The Offense of the Future*. By that time, Mouse had graduated and was coaching high school football in Oregon. "I stole his idea with the two slots and two wideouts," he admits. "But most of the similarities stop there. He still ran the ball more than we ever did. But most of the stuff we use has been stolen from somebody; it's just all been merged together in a workable, functioning package."

The single, biggest difference between the Mouse Davis Run 'n' Shoot and other look-alike versions is the route conversions. The routes change, depending on the coverage of the defense. It doesn't matter whether you're playing zone, man-to-man, man-under-zone, or whatever. Essentially, his receivers run where you aren't. The basic formation never changes; first-and-10, second-and-inches, or third-and-25. "We make the opposition defend the pass first, the run second," he preaches. "And just when we get you thinking about the pass, we open up the run. Our running game is successful simply by the element of surprise." Remarkably, the offense has only eight basic plays: five passing and three running.

After changing this and adjusting that, Davis unveiled his special offense in the early sixties at Milwaukie High School in Portland. He loves to tell the story over and over. "Wasn't a high school coach in the state that had ever even seen an offense like that," he laughs. "High school kids don't understand pass defense. We kinda took advantage of that." Always a victim of size himself, Mouse rigged his offense to cater to the undersized athlete; his receivers then, and now, are seldom over six feet tall, and often weigh less than 180 pounds. "My stature gave me a little more incentive," he admits. "There are a lot of blazing fast, great athletes who just aren't the stereotypical size of a football player, and never got a chance to play the game. This offense changed all that. If you can run, you can play for me."

As a high school coach, Davis won four league championships and a state title with the Run 'n' Shoot. He took his aerial circus to Portland State, where in 1975 he inherited a team with a

record of 57-76-1 since 1961 and a budget so small we rode buses
to nearly every away game and we never heard of a "pre-game
meal." PSU never granted full scholarships, just partial grants-in-
aid and other "creative financing" plans for athletes. Despite this
handicap (while playing against some schools with ninety scholarship players), his Portland State teams led the nation in passing
and total offense every year from 1975-80, averaging more than
5,000 yards per season and 35 points a game.

The school led the country in scoring three times, set twenty
NCAA Division I-AA offensive marks, and in my senior year,
1980, became the NCAA's all-time point producer, scoring 541
points in eleven games for a 49.2-point average. For three suc-
cessive years, we won national statistical championships, averaging 504.3 yards of total offense and 434.9 yards from 1978 to
1980.

June Jones was a perfect example of how Davis's confidence
could change your outlook. June had been a third- and fourth-
string quarterback at Oregon and Hawaii and in three years had
played only eleven downs of college football. After transferring to
Portland State to merely finish out scholastically and put football
behind him, June, a gangly, six-foot-four, 160-pounder, was
coaxed back to the playing field by Mouse. With Mouse and the
Run 'n' Shoot, June soared to national prominence, setting the
NCAA record for most yards passing—3,463—in a single season.
He threw forty-one touchdowns his senior year and was drafted
by the Atlanta Falcons, where he played six years. "Mouse's personality made me much more aggressive," says June, who served
two years as Mouse's offensive coordinator in the United States
Football League. "He brings out qualities in people they never
dreamed they had."

But Davis's determination and staunch belief in his offense led
to his undoing in 1981. After being hired as offensive coordinator
at the University of California, he refused to sway his way of offensive thinking when things didn't go just right early in the season. The head coach insisted Davis change to a more "reformed"
way of thinking. So Davis said good-bye, and took his show north
to the Canadian Football League, where he took over as offensive

coordinator in 1982 with the Toronto Argonauts. He promptly proved his bizarre strategy would work on the professional level. The Argonauts, perennial losers, reached the Grey Cup (league championship) game in 1982, then won it in 1983 with the offense. "All this time, we were perfecting the offense," he says. "Making it a little better, a little tighter."

The Run 'n' Shoot was running smoother than a high-tuned racing engine by 1983 when Mouse went to the now-defunct Houston Gamblers of the USFL. There he met Jim Kelly, a young, devil-be-damned rookie quarterback. Eighteen weeks later, Kelly had dwarfed Dan Marino's achievements, passing for a professional football record 5,219 yards and 44 touchdowns en route to leading the team to the Central Division title. The club established new all-time, single-season American professional marks for points (618), total net yards (7,684), passing yards (5,311), and touchdown passes (79). Davis took over the Denver franchise as head coach the next year, and despite having the lowest payroll in the league, took the team to the play-offs and finished second in the Western Conference.

So, clearly, his system works. But with him it's more than a system, more than a routine. It's the aura of Mouse Davis, the feeling of supreme confidence you get when you're around him. He gave that to me. It is important to understand Mouse in order to understand how I developed in four years as his college quarterback. He is all things to all people. He is entertaining, obviously, but he takes the time to be sincere. At Portland State, if you had to talk to him, his door was always open. He was never too busy. But he didn't do it for show; he didn't do it because a head coach was supposed to be like that. He did it because he enjoyed it. Mouse does things his way; he has a lot of pride in where he's come from. At PSU, he stayed within the rules, but he made it fun. Every player who ever played for Mouse considers him a friend. That's quite a feat.

The funny thing is that he's been criticized about his offense his entire career, despite the numbers and success it has had. He doesn't conform, and he never will, and that's what I love most about the man. The NFL is nothing but one guy copying another guy. That's why Mouse isn't an NFL head coach yet. A guy with fresh ideas scares the pants off the conservative NFL. He's had several offers to be an offensive coordinator for the NFL, but he's at the point in his career where he wants to run his own show. He is a leader, not a follower. He knows how good his system is, so he sticks to his guns. Davis was fifteen years ahead of his time when he was coaching high school kids. Long before the 49ers and the Broncos were using "read and react" pass routes, Mouse had high school and college kids like me doing it. He's a winner and he will win. He once told me,

> Usually, when coaches talk about discipline, they mean conformity. A disciplined pattern, to most coaches, is 18 yards and out-of-bounds every time. But discipline to me is different. The law, medicine, teaching—those are disciplines, callings where development of the basic tools leads to creativity. Conformity is fairly easy to have. But self-discipline is always to be worked for, in order to approach your potential. As a kid learns the tools of this offense, reading defenders and acting on the run, he can be more and more creative. That requires more discipline than rote offenses.

Mouse Davis made the game fun. Even though we had a lot of repetition in practice, he kept it from getting monotonous. The drills kept us fresh. We were always moving, always working. He would yell, but never did he hit a player or jerk face masks in dictator-type castigation. He was your coach, but first, he was your friend. During games, his intensity could burn holes through you. But during practice, he was very loose, very affable. "There's a time to work and a time to play," he quips.

A true optimist, Mouse supported his faith with hard work and belief in a way he knew was right. He stays up all night watching game films or devising written tests about the offense for his players to make sure every tiny detail is understood. He teaches you a lot about yourself, about respect, heart, and all the other intangibles that make you a winner. I visited him several times after he went to the USFL, and it was still the same, just like the days at Portland State. All his players still use the same words to describe him: fatherlike, patient, loving, but hard as nails if you ever betray him. A great communicator, Mouse explained things so well, so clearly, that he proved the game doesn't have to be as complicated as everyone thinks it does. That's why I loved the Run 'n' Shoot.

So, after receiving Coach Davis's offer of a grant-in-aid, I contacted him and we agreed to talk in person. He invited me to lunch at Roses, a favorite spot for delicious pastries and giant sandwiches. Mouse burst into the room, and from the time we shook hands, his wide-eyed charisma cut right through me. His loud laugh, though boisterous, was relaxing. "You're a pretty big kid," he acknowledged, tabbing me with a nickname he would use for the next four years. "Your high school coach tells me you gotta heckuva arm if you could ever get a chance to use it." He bellowed with laughter, which made me laugh, too. The appeal of his car-salesman charm and honest-to-God sincerity was irresistible.

"Hey, big kid, if you're ever going to be something in college as a quarterback, you've got to put horseradish on your roast beef," he instructed when the waitress delivered our orders. "Got to pour it on, nice and thick." His eyes sparkled, and my silence told him instantly I was a horseradish rookie. Obediently, I buried my sandwich in horseradish, a sure indication I wanted to be a college success.

Seconds later, with tears streaming down my red face, and tears of laughter streaming down his, my mind was made up. To top it off, Coach Davis, to be funny, even stuck me with the tip. I loved the guy.

"Thanks for the meal, Coach Davis," I said afterward.

He grabbed my shoulder, eyes widening.

"Hey, big kid," he said smiling, "my name is Mouse."

My dad noticed the excitement in my eyes when I got home, and it didn't take us long to confirm my decision. "You've got a good opportunity here, son," he said. "You're the fifth-string quarterback, but you need to make up your mind." I did. I would attend PSU, a 17,000-student commuter school just outside Portland's downtown business district.

It was unbelievable that a long-shot, running quarterback like me from a small, local high school was going to get an opportunity to be ringmaster of the Mouse Davis aerial circus.

That night I lay in bed imagining myself as quarterback of the Portland State Vikings with a coach named Mouse. For several hours I was too excited to even shut my eyes.

Mouse, indeed. Chuckling, I drifted off to sleep.

4

College Daze

"... only a few persons influence the formation of our character; the multitude pass us by like a distant army. One friend, one teacher, one beloved ... are the means by which his nation and the spirit of his nation affect the individual."

—Richter

"There's only two kinds of young quarterbacks in the world. One gets better when you put him in the game. The other gets worse."

—Darrell "Mouse" Davis

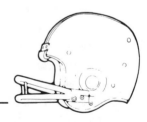

"Get up, Mike. Get uppp!" Mouse Davis's eyes were riveted on fallen Portland State quarterback Mike Atwood who had just disappeared under a wave of bodies. Thunder rumbled in the background, and the dark evening skies at Portland's Civic Stadium grew ominous. The rain started again, sweeping across the field in sheets. Atwood, a senior, climbed unsteadily to his feet, leaning on Joel Sigel, our big running back. Limping slowly, he came toward the sideline. Mouse shook his head. The rain turned his windbreaker a slick green; water dripped from his nose and chin. His concern about our 3–4 record—and the importance of this game against Oregon College of Education—was reflected in the tautness of his face.

I stood quietly behind him, arms crossed and shivering in the cold wind and rain. A few weeks ago none of the receivers had even wanted to play catch with me before practice, because my fluttering airballs seldom found their mark. Under Mouse's Run 'n' Shoot system, however, even fifth-string, freshmen quarterbacks got a lot of work in practice. Inch-by-inch, I had worked my way up to second string. I beat out Curt Howard and Mark Neffendorf, then Tim Piggot broke his leg.

Suddenly, I was second string.

"Feels like a pulled muscle, Mouse," Atwood groaned when he reached the sideline, his face distorted with pain. Mouse whipped around to me. His eyes were slits as rain danced on his face. His easy smile was gone. Maybe he was thinking of the miracles that June Jones, our nationally ranked quarterback, had regularly produced a year ago. But June was gone now, graduated into the National Football League. I snapped my chin strap.

"Show time, big kid," Mouse said. "This is your chance to line it up and go. It's your time to prove to me and everybody else that you can do it. It's your show."

He slapped me on the butt as I trotted onto the field. His lips were pressed tightly over gritted teeth, not for the moment chewing his ever-present wad of gum. We didn't huddle in a circle, but instead lined up in two rows. Linemen stood in the back, "itty-bitty guys," as Mouse called them, were in the front, and I stood facing the entire team. The feeling was similar to directing a choir without having any music lessons.

"Let's get it together out here," I said, my voice showing no trace of the nervousness that knotted my stomach.

We ran a few plays to end the first half, which was all I needed to get rid of the butterflies, and went to the locker room with a slim 7–6 lead.

"Kid, you understand what you're doing?" Mouse asked at the

half, wiping rainwater off his face. He scribbled some route changes on the blackboard. "Piece of cake," he said. "Let's take it to these guys."

I went out, somehow sure we could take it to them. In the second half, it all came together. I felt in command of the offense. I was seeing the things Mouse had been telling me I would see. On one play the whole field seemed to open up like the Red Sea. With the coolness of a veteran, I waited until the last second to release the ball, then—with everything I had in my arm—I fired a 73-yard bomb to Dave Stief, who was running away from everybody. I jumped up and down with my hands raised as I saw Dave take it in for the score.

Mouse beamed when I came off the field. "Easy, huh kid?" he asked, smiling. By the fourth quarter, we were moving the ball at will. I was actually recognizing defenses. Minutes later, receiver John Colasurdo, who was nicknamed Rocky after the character on the Bullwinkle Show, broke between two defenders; with a snap I drilled the ball to him. He shook off one tackler, juked another, and ran the distance for an 82-yard touchdown. "Atta babies," Mouse yelled, hugging his players as we came panting off. He turned to Colasurdo. "You sure can fly for a little pooper." His eyes twinkled. We roared with laughter.

When the gun sounded, we had won 34–22. In less than three quarters of play, I had completed fourteen out of twenty-six passes for 374 yards and 3 touchdowns. That stormy Oregon evening was the real start of my college football career. I took over for Mike Atwood, who eventually quit the team. My chance crossing with Mouse became, I think, one of the most unique relationships between a head coach and a quarterback. For the next three years, I was an extension of the Mouse Davis system, taking his ideas off the chalkboard and transforming them into reality on the field. And through the whole game, I never even noticed the rain.

Stuart Gaussoin, meanwhile, had been playing at local Clackamas Community (Junior) College. I lived at home my freshman

year, but Stu got himself a little place at Clackamas. Our friendship and rivalry that year washed in and out like the tide. We saw
each other regularly, but there was an element of wariness, maybe
envy.

The week after I became a starter, Stu invited me over to his
apartment. "How 'bout getting me a shot at Portland State?" Stu
asked. He had been hinting for some time about the possibility
but now he was getting emphatic. "I know I can play there." I
agreed to talk to Mouse again.

"No way, Neil," Mouse said the next morning behind the little
wooden desk in his tiny office, which was covered with game
films, charts, diagrams, and other paraphernalia. "Look, I saw
both you kids in high school. You were both good, but you had
size. Sure, we like small kids here, but Stu is too small."

"But Mouse, just give him a chance. If he doesn't work out, at
least you tried."

Mouse shook his head. "We'll see," he said. I smiled as I stood
up to walk out. "Hey, kid—no promises!" he yelled behind me.

Stu played on Saturday afternoons and we played on Saturday
nights, so I'd often take a group of teammates over to Clackamas
to watch him play. And I kept bugging Mouse about him. Stu's
success started getting Mouse's attention. He was catching everything thrown in his direction and quickly established himself as
their best receiver and kickoff returner.

Off the field, meanwhile, Stu was still as good at making passes
as he was at catching them. And I kind of envied his social ease.
College parties were a first for both of us, and university life was
opening doors to other worlds. Girls were more mature and aggressive, and alcohol and marijuana, the only drug I remember
seeing in college, were always present. Stuart, although short, had
developed into a handsome, rugged guy. I was still more of a gan-
gling, awkward kid, unrefined and lacking culture. The ladies
were attracted to Stu, and I got several dates just from riding
along on his coattails. Although I attended parties, I often felt
strange about it and I was conscious of not compromising my
Christian principles. If I was in the wrong place at the wrong
time, people would talk. And I didn't want my witness to be un-

dercut by people thinking I was doing something wrong on the side, remembering the lesson I'd learned in high school.

After that second-half performance against Oregon College, the media, which had ignored the second-stringer all year, all wanted to talk to me. Mouse immediately named me the starting quarterback for the next game at home against the University of Puget Sound, marking the first time in his three years as a college coach he had started a freshman. "You've earned it," Mouse told me. My parents were excitedly clipping every word from the newspapers as I headed toward my first college start.

The Wednesday before the game I came home exhausted from school and practice. I flopped into a chair. "Look what Mouse said about you," my mother said, handing me a clip from the *Oregon Journal.* I was pleasantly surprised.

> "He has the strongest freshman arm I've ever seen," Davis says of Neil Lomax, the kid out of Lake Oswego High School who is suiting up for his ninth collegiate game. "He has touch, range, and accuracy."

By Saturday, I was raring to go. My parents had told everybody that "my boy is starting tonight," and many of my old high school friends were in attendance. My stomach was churning when we took the field, but once the game started, all was forgotten but the job at hand. On the third play from scrimmage I called a "Rip Scramble Right." Settling back to pass, I could see Dave Stief, a tall, scrappy guy, running a corner route. Just as he made his break I burned the ball between two UPS defenders. Dave made a great catch and ran the last 10 yards to the end zone for our first score of the night. From that point I possessed a confidence I'd never felt. I just believed we were unstoppable. I came right back and hit Mike Hanacek for a 57-yard touchdown. I was just amazed by the potential of the offense. Quarterbacking the Run 'n' Shoot is like riding a rocket; it rumbles and rumbles, then eventually explodes. We won, 63–9, and I finished with 359 yards and 5 touchdowns, and no interceptions.

The next week we bused up to Canada where we beat Simon Frazier College, 55–13, and the excitement among the players was incredible. When we took the field for the final game against Montana State, we knew there was absolutely no way we could lose. "I know you guys are feeling pretty high right now," Mouse said in the locker room before we went out. "But I want everybody to concentrate, do their jobs, and have fun. Most of all, have fun." Did we ever. I completed forty-one of fifty-nine aerials for 469 yards and a school record 6 touchdowns as we beat Montana State 56–35. At the time, they were the reigning Division I-AA national champions. They scored just frequently enough for Mouse to keep us starters in the game.

Sammy Holland, then Montana State's head coach, approached me afterward.

"Good game," he said. I shook his hand and thanked him. "I have one question for you," he added. "Didn't your arm ever get sore? If we threw our guy that much, his arm would fall off."

We finished the year 7–4, after starting 0–3, and within a month I had become the boy wonder of Portland.

And my arm was in no danger of falling off; if anything, it was getting stronger.

My relationship with Christ continued to grow, despite the fact that I fell down on occasion. I used my newfound popularity with the media to share the love of Jesus as I had in high school. The only difference was now I had a bigger audience. Though I wasn't a street-corner prophet, I was kind of aggressive about my faith. My teammates were a captive audience, and I tried to tell them about the Lord. In the fast-paced world of college athletics, there was a tendency to put the Lord down, and I overemphasized the importance—to everybody—of keeping Christ first. This included my habit of passing out cards with Bible verses on them. But the respect of the seniors was a little harder to come by in the locker room than on the field. I was involved with two fellowship groups during my college career. Our team trainer, Leo Marty, a meek, soft-spoken, and dedicated Christian man, headed up the team's Fellowship of Christian Athletes chapter. Later, I participated in weekly Bible studies that were led by Al

Egg, a Portland businessman who fulfilled the spiritual needs of our team through the reading of the Word.

Early in my college career, my overzealousness for Christ led me to Mouse's office, however.

"Kid," he said, taking a deep breath, "you've got to cool it a little bit on the religion stuff. A couple of the other kids have been by my office and said that you're making too big a deal of religion as a team concept. We all understand that everyone has their own beliefs, but I have to treat everyone fairly. It all has to happen for each person in his own way. We don't need Christianity to become a diversion on this ball club. Understand?"

I shook my head yes. Mouse wasn't a Christian, but he was perceptive about such issues.

"Coach," I said, "I'm proud of my faith. I just want to do whatever I can to help other people."

"I'm very aware of that, Neil. Just don't wear it on your sleeve or wear us out with it. Let people see it, instead of telling them all the time. You relax and they'll relax."

Without admitting it, neither of us had given in; rather, we had both compromised to some degree. Mouse, because of his pride and determination, admires those same traits in someone else, and he respected me for taking a stand before my teammates. In a way, he taught me the value of being a team player, but didn't ridicule me for my faith. I learned to show rather than preach my faith, and it never again presented a problem. I'd rather force a football down someone's throat than the Bible.

In fact, weeks later Mouse told the *Oregonian* that, "because of Lomax's religious convictions, he has a lot of self-confidence. He's not the kind of kid who is going to panic under pressure. He strongly feels that his faith helps him. It does."

Late spring in 1978 was a time of reckoning. I was clearly cementing myself as the starting quarterback during spring drills. Stuart, meanwhile, whom Mouse had agreed to "take a look at," was proving he belonged on this team. My constant badgering and his obvious talents earned him a starting slotback position

going into the fall. And off the field, my world champion Trail
Blazers clinched the Pacific Division crown in the NBA and were
making a move—behind most valuable player Bill Walton—on
another league title. I was on top of the world.

The complexion of my parents' scrapbooks were beginning to
change. Pictures of Mitch doing his dance routines in high school,
clips of Valorie's high school basketball heroics were slowly being
covered up by all the freshly snipped publicity the Portland
media was devoting to me. I was a little caught up in it myself.
Though it didn't happen all the time, it was quite a novelty to
walk into a restaurant and have someone point or whisper, "Hey
... isn't that Neil Lomax, that freshman who broke those
records?" Meanwhile, my parents continued clipping every word
about me from the local papers.

I moved out of the house after my freshman year, taking a tiny
apartment on campus with Stu and Randy Hunt, another teammate. My parents didn't like the idea, but it was important to me
to be closer to the school. It allowed me more time to practice,
more time to study, and relieved me of the pressures my parents
subconsciously placed on me. I just needed my freedom. They
weren't doing it intentionally, but they seemed more affected by
my achievements than I did. As all good parents would, they
wanted to constantly share in my good fortune; they wanted to
hear about every practice, every day at school. Their attention
made me self-conscious and embarrassed, and carrying a full load
and playing football allows little leftover time for debriefing sessions with your folks every evening.

Ron Kincaid, however, was not swayed by my newfound success. Church events played a big role in my life, and Ron capitalized on every opportunity to remind me of my priorities. Not in a
chastising, rebuking sort of way, but in a kind, friendly manner.
With just a single question, Ron had a way of making me reeval-
uate myself and my thinking.

"Hey, Neil," he'd ask, "who have you been trying to bring to
the Lord lately?" Wow. But he wouldn't stop there.

"Anybody in particular you've been ministering to?"

Such questions hit like a ton of bricks and forced me to keep my focus on other people, not myself.

My sophomore season helped humble me. We were a young team, and the senior leadership that had carried me through the last few games my freshman year was gone. Mouse worked us harder than ever in practice, but as the season drew nearer things just didn't seem to be coming together. All the things that had magically meshed at the tail end of the previous season crumbled during the early days of September 1978. Reading defenses, which I thought was so simple, now was as clear as mud. Long touchdowns were dropped. Easy handoffs were fumbled. The problem wasn't the Run 'n' Shoot system, it was our execution of it. Mouse preached execution. "When we execute, nobody in football can stop us," he'd yell. "Believe in this system. It works. Only you, and you alone, can stop this team."

But our charade of the Bad News Bears in football gear continued, much to Mouse's chagrin. We were filing into the locker room after a 42–14 opening game beating at the hands of Northern Arizona when a reporter stopped Mouse outside the door.

"What about Lomax?"

Mouse never hesitated. "Lomax is gonna be one of the greatest quarterbacks we've ever had," he said. "Don't judge him on one game, or the rest of this team for that matter. This is gonna be a helluva club. And Lomax, trust me, is gonna be great."

He believed, when there was no reason to. Nor did we give him one. Injuries began felling the offense like cordwood. I sustained broken ribs myself, and Mouse took it upon himself to locate and purchase a flak jacket that would save my ribs from further pounding. I don't know where he found the money to buy such an expensive piece of equipment, because it certainly wasn't available in our budget. Heading into our fourth game against Sacramento State, we were 1–2 and had been outscored over three games 85–54, a rarity for a Mouse-coached team. But against Sacramento, we exploded. I played less than a half but completed twenty of twenty-nine for 261 yards, and scored 5 touchdowns—4 passing and 1 running. Stu, however, wasn't as lucky. Early in the game he dove for a long ball, and his shoulder took the brunt of the impact and became dislocated. But the final score of 63–7 helped relieve some of his pain.

The rest of the year was exhausting. Our record slid to 4–6, and we nearly lost the final game of the season against South Dakota. Tied 21–21 with two and a half minutes left to play, it seemed we were on the verge of blowing another victory. But then in the next two minutes I threw 3 touchdowns and we blew them out, 42–21. I finished the game with 376 yards. Throwing close to 400 yards a game was becoming common for me. My 3,506 yards passing that season had fallen 12 yards short of June Jones's school record of 3,518. *Not bad,* I thought. But we still had finished the year 5–6, handing Mouse the first—and last— losing season in his coaching career with the Run 'n' Shoot.

Since my days of "broadcasting" my own games in the backyard, I had aspired to be an announcer. So at Portland State, I began to prepare for such a career. At the time I really never considered pro football as an alternative, so I worked hard, planning for life after college football. Speech classes were my favorite, and I enjoyed the podium. I could and would talk about anything. If anyone felt nervous, it was probably my audience wondering when I was going to shut up.

But my favorite professor and speech teacher, Ben Padro, would admonish me, "Neil, the audience is never fooled by lack of preparation." Gradually I learned to think on my feet, not just talk.

I took pride in my schoolwork and strived to graduate in four years. I also applied for—and received—a Basic Educational Opportunity Grant, which meant I wasn't costing the school anything. The federal grant was designed to aid lower-income students, and my living away from home helped me obtain the financing for school. I figured Mouse needed all the school money he could get to keep the team stocked with able freshmen. I was quite proud of the way I combined my schooling with my football demands.

Mouse recognized which of his athletes were brighter than others. Although he never cheated with grades, he would direct the less-able players to easier classes. "Get your degrees," he would say. "One way or another, an honest degree will mean more down the road than virtually anything you can do." I would get furious at players who had scholastic opportunities and were simply too lazy to take advantage of them. Sure, it's hard, but to not get the full academic credit is just plain stupid.

Kids around the campus were starting to recognize me, and that introduced a new phase in my life which is still very important to me today. Hanging around downtown Portland, I'd see little boys and girls recognize me, then hang back like they were afraid to talk to me. But it meant a lot to have kids—or adults—come up to me and shake my hand. It made my day when people would approach me and say, "Hey, I really enjoy watching you play." I made it a point never to be too busy to stop and sign an autograph for a kid. With children, you often have only one opportunity to make an impression. They leave either thinking you're a nice guy or a real jerk. There's no middle ground. I'm very sensitive to that.

In 1979, my brother Mitch transferred from Oregon State to Portland State and was beginning to feel the call of God on his life. I talked to Mitch a lot, and the influence Christ had in his life was mesmerizing.

One evening Mitch was stretched out on my sofa when he began to hint about the ministry. He had been considering a career in business administration, but it was obvious that he didn't have his heart in it, despite his solid grades.

"Neil, the thing I love doing the most is just telling folks about Jesus," he said, his eyes staring at the ceiling. "I love to tell people what a difference Jesus can make in their lives, and how much love He has for everyone."

"So," I answered bluntly. "What are you gonna do about it?"

A lot of people who had known the "old Mitch" already found the new one hard to accept. His announcement that he would probably go to seminary after graduation made it even harder.

By now, Terry, who had enrolled at Portland State, and Val,

were thriving Christians. Like Mitch, they were always willing to share their faith, and people knew that to talk to them or befriend them would mean hearing about Christ. While this removed them from the popular crowd, it helped them develop a core of true, believing friends.

Because we were all believers, we wanted our folks to be, too. During the time all us kids were going through life-changing experiences, Mom professed her faith. But Dad made no such claim. Rather, he openly resisted us whenever the subject arose. So on one particular day Terry and Mitch decided to take him to lunch at a Pizza Hut and force-feed him the gospel with his pizza.

Mitch recounted the tale to me afterward, and I shook my head. Both my brothers had taken their big King James Bibles into the restaurant and had come on pretty hard, pumping Dad with Scripture in front of everybody. "Dad," Mitch had said, pointing out John 3:16, "you're going to hell. Dad, you're going to hell unless you ask Jesus into your heart."

My dad refused to swallow any of the message, or the pizza. Instead, he became colder. "You guys haven't got me yet," he doggedly told Mitch and Terry.

Mitch was distraught that evening. "What was I thinking about, Neil?" he asked. The pain was evident in his eyes. He hated to see Dad unsaved.

"What a way to welcome Dad into the kingdom," he sighed.

I didn't know how to comfort Mitch. In fact, I couldn't even think of any suggestions as to how to reach my parents. My dad had been great, especially when we were young. Coaching our Little League teams, building stuff for us in the yard, Dad was always trying to put smiles on our faces. He knew nothing about baseball, but he tried. He hurt when we hurt, he cried when we cried, he laughed when we laughed. But when we got to high school, he started to kind of drift away. Each of us kids feels there were different reasons for his withdrawal from the family, but I believe that he just was no longer getting the satisfaction out of his job, out of his life, that he once had. It was sad. His life no longer fulfilled him; it was no longer important to him. Conflicts between him and Mom arose frequently, and I remember talking to Terry and Mitch once about the possibilities of them getting a divorce. It scared us. The tension was always there, at least, I felt it.

Then my football career began to emerge and it seemed to hold their relationship together. The only time they seemed to be happy was when they were caught up in the midst of this game or that game, or this record or that record. It was as if they saw my success as a kind of escape from their lives.

As we prepared for the fall of 1979, Mouse was more intense than ever. We ran until we couldn't run, threw until we couldn't throw. The pressure was mounting. The "young kids" of two years ago had come of age, and the PSU administration was expecting big things of Mouse. The pressure on me was building at an incredible pace. With the season months away, the papers were already hyping "what if" possibilities, based on achievements in my sophomore year. It was very distracting, but Mouse was pretty good at keeping our minds on the game.

Summer practice opened to a sweltering Portland sun and the heat that simmered off the turf at Civic Stadium offered no relief. Mouse was more relentless than the sun, however.

"You wanna goof off?" he screamed to a group of linemen who were slowing down during sprint drills. "You wanna be lazy? Fine. We'll run five more. And think about being lazy while you run these."

He ran our fannies off. Mouse loved reaction drills. He would line up the defense, then get down in front of them in a three-point stance. "Don't move till I drop my hat," he'd order. Jump offsides, and you were running ten extra sprints. We were never the biggest or the baddest, but we didn't make fundamental mistakes. Mouse figured if his team could be the most mentally prepared team on the field, then more often than not brains would win over brawn. Too bad more pro teams can't realize that.

A quarterback's cadence and inflection are very important in a game. And Mouse got a real kick out of teaching his quarterbacks how to control the inflection in their voices when calling the signals. It really made his day.

"Hard count, Neil, hard count," he'd shout. "Like this. Reeeeaddddy ... settttttt ... huuuuuuuut ... hut, hut ... huuuut ... hut."

At the end of practice, we'd all run. Being a quarterback, I had spent my first two years running with the other backs. Unfortunately, running with the "itty bitty guys" meant having to kill myself to keep up with them. By my junior year, I'd learned to lag behind and run with the offensive linemen. They were slower, so I could coast. But Mouse drove everybody hard.

"Let's see my little bitty babies on the line," he'd yell, blowing his whistle. "Get up there, you little babies. Let's see some speed out there. You know I love you, but don't make us have to do it again."

Before my junior year, I moved into a little house in a Portland suburb with Stu, Jeff Urness, and Robin Pflugrad. Robin was a well-muscled wide receiver, who, though not as flashy as Stu, was the epitome of the work ethic. He was the Raymond Berry of small college football: methodical, deliberate, studious and one of the best guys you'll ever meet. The four of us had developed a pretty fast friendship, but sharing rent on a house is risky whenever four young men are involved. One evening we were watching the Seattle Supersonics battle it out with the Washington Bullets on a fuzzy black-and-white TV, when Jeff mumbled that the phone bill hadn't been paid as usual. "Money will be the ruin of our cozy, adultlike relationship," he said. We all threw pillows at him, calling him a prophet of doom. Little did we know.

Soon fights were erupting over such crises as, "Who took my steak?" or, "Who drank my milk?" or, "Who hasn't paid his share of the electric bill?" Robin was the most humble, seldom complained, and was never late with his payments. But the rest of us wreaked havoc on one another. It was obvious our junior year was going to be a memorable one, if for no other reason than the constant battles on the homestead.

The season was a week away, and I picked up a paper on my

way home. The headline *Is Lomax for Real?* jumped off the page at me. "These guys are making too big a deal of this," I told Jeff, who was our best defensive back, as I opened the refrigerator and took a swig of apple juice with a hint of 7-Up, my favorite mixed drink. "I've had some success, but these guys are blowing it out of proportion."

Jeff shook his head. "You never know, Neil," he said. "You never know."

I wiped my mouth and glanced back down at the story:

Statistics say that by the time Neil Lomax is out of college in 1980, he will be the most prolific passer in the college game.

Good grief. *It sure would be nice,* I thought, *if they'd let me play my junior season before they start making such claims.* My mind began wandering, though, as I considered the impact of the prediction. "Most prolific passer in the college game. . . ."

I smiled to myself. *You never know.*

5

Test of Success

"If one advances confidently in the direction of his dreams, and endeavors to live the life which he has imagined, he will meet with a success unexpected in common hours."

—Henry David Thoreau

Mouse was screaming, but the referees weren't listening. "There are twelve men on the field," he yelled. "Twelve men. Twelve , somebody count them." Mouse was livid. Ripping the headset right off his head and slamming it into the damp, spongy turf, he roared up and down the sideline, frantically waving his arms. Northern Arizona quarterback Brian Potter had hit shifty receiver Ken Jenkins with a 21-yard scoring pass as time ran out in our season opener, and although we still led 21–20, we could only stand by helplessly on the sidelines as they went for the 2-point conversion and the victory.

Problem was, Mouse had counted twelve men on the field— they had three guys in the backfield, which was one too many. Potter took the snap and wheeled, handing the ball off to his full-back. The "twelfth man" led the back into the hole, and the other back fell through for the winning conversion.

Mouse clutched his head with both hands, then ran across the field to verbally attack the back judge. "You're the worst official I've ever seen in all my years of football," he said confronting the tall referee. "Can you count?"

The referee warned him, but Mouse didn't back down. He hated losing, especially in part by an official's error. "Turn me in," he said. "My kids play their hearts out, then lose because you can't count." I'd never seen Mouse so ticked off.

The ride back to our apartment resembled a funeral proces-sion. Although I'd had a decent game—3 touchdowns—this year was starting out just like the last. But something way down deep had been worked into us; we remained optimistic. With Mouse, you stay optimistic.

The next week in practice, I sustained my first college injury when I chipped a bone in my left ankle and tore some minor liga-ments. As luck would have it, however, we had a bye that week, and—with a good tape job on my left ankle—I was ready to play by the time we traveled to Weber State. We beat them on a field goal, 16–13, then lost a heartbreaker to Humboldt State, 30–29. But the offense was taking off. "We're moving the ball," Mouse would say. "But so is the other team."

My third year in the offense, I was getting very comfortable with everything Mouse was asking me to do. I would see things on the field and change the play, and Mouse would grab me by the shoulder afterward and say, "What on earth did you think you saw out there?" So I'd tell him. Then we'd watch the films, and 90 percent of the time, I'd be right. Mouse would wink at me. He could sense the whole package coming together in my mind.

When Puget Sound came into Portland on October 6, 1979, a new era dawned on Portland State football. For the first time in over a year, everything clicked. Our receivers turned their defensive backs inside out, our offensive linemen pass-blocked like professionals, and I just did what I'd been taught to do. Zip, zip, zip, we moved down the field at will. I finished nineteen of thirty for 305 yards and 6 touchdowns, becoming Portland State's career leader for touchdowns (53), passing yards (6,263), and total offense (6,323). I also led the NCAA in total offense, averaging 275.2 yards per game, and had thrown 10 touchdowns.

We whipped Cal State-Northridge, 34–21, before traveling to Northern Colorado. Again, the offense lit up the sky, but we couldn't get it into the end zone. It was a classic case of overconfidence on my part, and I tried time after time to force passes I shouldn't even have considered. We lost, 21–20, despite having thrown the ball seventy-nine times. I completed forty-four passes for 499 yards; all PSU and NCAA I-AA records. But I threw five interceptions. Monday morning I found myself in Mouse's office again.

"Come in, Neil," he said. "Sit down."

For several minutes he said nothing; he just flipped through page after page of statistics from Saturday night. I fidgeted nervously, stared at the floor, glanced out the door, and picked my nails.

Finally, he rested his coyote eyes on me.

"You played like horsecrap." His eyes bored right through me, never blinking. "That was one of the worst individual performances I've ever seen from you. You got something else on your mind? Something I need to know about?"

I was stunned; I didn't know what to say. Mouse had a way of keeping even the best players humble. For a second, I wanted to blurt out that I'd set division records for touchdowns, yards passing, and everything else. But there was no retort to those eyes, which were searching me for an answer. I decided the best thing to do, the most Christian thing to do, would be to concede. After all, he was right. I had been too cocky. I had been forcing passes.

"You're right, Mouse," I said, hanging my head. "Sorry."

To this day, Mouse remembers that. It was a painful lesson for me, but I realized sometimes the biggest statement you can make is "I'm sorry . . . I'll try again."

Meanwhile, Stuart was having an incredible year. By now, Mouse was happy to accept credit for the "discovery" of Stuart Gaussoin. Stu and I were doing everything together, on and off the field. To me, however, the most irritating thing about Stu was his dislike of practice and his constant aches and pains. We all had them, but his were always worse than everyone else's. Midway through practice sessions a sharp blast from Mouse's whistle would bring us all to a halt. Somewhere, trainers would be tending to Stuart, who was suffering from a "sore" leg, a bruised finger, or something. Always something. It almost got to be funny. The entire team would be loosening up prior to practice when Stu would come out with an obvious limp. And man, could he limp. The wincing he'd practiced for years on his mother ("But I'm too sick to go to school") had developed into the best pained expression in all of college football.

"Problem, Stu?" I'd ask, stretching my own tired muscles. Stu would limp around, grab this thigh or that calf or whatever, then explain.

"Nasty bruise, Neil," he'd say. Mouse would amble over.

"Feeling rough, kid?" Mouse would inquire.

"Pretty bad, Mouse," he'd answer, his limp worsening. "I'd better sit this one out. Want to be ready for Saturday."

So the entire team would continue, lumps and all, while Stuart watched from the sidelines or ran lightly on his own. He hated the work, and pain, that accompanied football. But when Saturday came around, any complaints that had been voiced during the week were silenced by his performance. Stu could do things most receivers only dream about, which poses a pretty good argument for how good he could've been if he had worked harder.

Stu talked frequently about getting a shot in the pros in a few years. I dreamed about it too, but I knew that coming up from

PSU, a "minor-league" school, made it very unlikely. But Stu would ramble on and on. Yet, with the success we were having, I couldn't really fault him for thinking about it. Stu would often mention the money that could be made in professional football.

"If things work out, I'd like to give the pros a try," he said. "I'm sure nobody's looking at me, but I'd like to satisfy myself that I gave it a shot. I'm not afraid to fail."

To say I wasn't aware of the records would be lying. The week before, against San Francisco State, I had surpassed NCAA major-college career passing yardage and total offense leader Jack Thompson of Washington State (the Division I-A passing leader) and Gene Swick of Toledo (the total offense leader of I-A). With a convincing 37–10 victory, we had improved our record to 4–4, although our defeats had come by a total of 6 points.

With three games to play, Stuart led the nation in receptions with 81 for 1,054 yards and 8 touchdowns, while my 2,887 yards put me 1,004 yards ahead of any challengers in college football. The victory over San Francisco State earned Mouse and me our first appearance in *Sports Illustrated*; on page 68, before the entire country, I stood there behind Mouse with a big grin on my face.

Bart Wright, a columnist with the *Oregonian*, approached me after practice the week before the Idaho State game. I was standing on the sideline, winging passes to Stu.

"Whadda you think about playing pro ball?" he asked us.

Stu's eyes lit up. I just smirked as, grunting, I flipped another spiral to Stu.

"Bart," I said, "I have my faith in God as a very real part of my life, so I think I'll be all right, even if the pros don't want me."

It wasn't the answer Bart was expecting. My heart told me I wanted to be a pro, but it was hard to get carried away with guys like Ron Kincaid always holding you accountable. In Saturday's paper, Bart accurately reflected my feelings, but at the same time reminded me of what could be on the horizon:

> ... the figurative leader of the Christian athlete movement is Neil Lomax, the junior quarterback of Portland State University. While Lomax is quick to share the praise, he's done much

of it on his own. Three years ago, he was the quarterback in a run-oriented offense at Lake Oswego High School.

Today, he's on the doorstep of NCAA history.

We normally drew crowds of about six thousand to venerable Civic Stadium, where one scribe wrote, "the artificial turf is growing shiny between 40s . . . there they throw and throw until the receivers have run three miles of imaginative patterns; until Lomax begins to list to the right, his throwing arm swinging two inches lower than his left." On the night of the Idaho State game, more than ten thousand were on hand.

Although our team was the Vikings, our mascot was none other than a giant Mouse, played by my brother Terry. When Terry had on the Mouse outfit, he was outrageous. Hilarious. His personality took on another side. He would cavort around the stadium in ridiculous fashion, and the roars of the crowd were evidence of their love for his antics. While we warmed up for Idaho State, I caught myself laughing as I watched Terry carry on for the home crowd.

The game went fast. We were throwing almost every down, and despite trying not to think about it, I knew I was closing in on some all-time records. Midway through the third quarter, I flipped a little 7-yarder to slotback Kenny Johnson. The roar from the crowd was deafening, and I was confused before the reality of the moment sunk in.

"Folks, Neil Lomax, the big quarterback from Lake Oswego, has just passed for an NCAA, all-time, all-division total offense mark," praised PSU public relations director and radio announcer Larry Sellers from his perch in the booth. "With two games and a season left for the big kid, Lomax has 8,425 yards total offense as a collegian and is within 170 yards of the NCAA career passing mark, held by Abilene Christian's Jim Lindsey, which he set in 1967–70."

I couldn't believe all the microphones being stuck in my face after the game, which we won by a 44–14 tally. With my wet hair sticking out in every direction and a towel slung around my bare shoulders, I could hardly catch my breath.

"I'm happy with the record, and equally amazed," I blurted. Writers scribbled on their note pads, flashbulbs blinded me, and sportscasters all jockeyed for elbow room. "It's just now beginning to soak in," I continued. "I tried not to think about all that record stuff, but it was there. I'm glad it's over, but I'm glad the team knows it had a part in everything I did."

But it didn't end there. The next week we faced the Montana Grizzlies, and there was electricity in the air as the crowd filed in for more Run 'n' Shoot heroics. Mouse had put fun back in football, and it was taking Portland by storm.

"Some crowd, eh, Stu?" Helmets pushed back on our heads, we watched as the thousands poured into the stadium. It was the biggest crowd we'd ever played for.

"Long way from Lake Oswego." Stu's words rang in my ears. "Long, long way from L.O." Stu dropped his voice to a whisper. "It seems like yesterday."

Our reminiscing was ended by the opening kickoff, and the Grizzlies made it clear they weren't planning to roll over and play dead. But again the offense dictated to the defense, instead of the other way around. Just before halftime, I completed a quick inside route for a first down over the middle; it set the record for most NCAA career yards passing. Ever. The crowd was screaming in pandemonium.

"Atta baby, Neil," Stuart said, hugging me as I stared blankly at the crowd. "Stu, man," I said, "can you believe this?"

"You did it, baby," he answered. "Just like Mouse said."

On the sidelines Terry, in the giant Mouse suit, was smashing old phonograph records to symbolize the moment. Every flip, every record that smashed to pieces, every movement by the "Big Mouse" drove the fans to an even higher frenzy.

Ten pairs of eyes were all staring at me. I turned to look at Mouse from mid-field to get the next play. Our eyes met in tranquil communication, oblivious to the noise and confusion swirling around us. He grinned for a second, motioned in the next play, then rubbed a hand through his hair. He turned away.

For the last three years, all Mouse had asked for was cooperation. Don't try to figure it out, he would say. Just believe. Don't try to solve the riddles. Just believe, baby, just believe. He had asked me to run the most unorthodox offense in football. His offense. His entire career he had waited for this moment. He had been laughed at, scoffed at, and ridiculed for his "undisciplined, circus-style" offense. Against Montana, his offense did what no offense had ever done before it.

The Run 'n' Shoot had come of age.

We closed the season 6–5, and profiles of Mouse and me were popping up in newspapers and sports shows around the nation. The records were amazing: total offensive yardage per season and career (3,966 and 9,188), all-division passing yardage per season and career (3,950 and 9,126), and total completions per season (299). I had set or tied sixteen passing records and fifteen total offense marks. Stuart, meanwhile, had caught ninety passes for 1,132 yards, both NCAA receiving records, and his game average of 125.8 yards was also a record. The media labeled us the "Oswego Pass Connection."

The last few days of the season held new surprises. I was chosen Little All-American by the Mizlou TV network and was presented with the Haywood Award, given to Oregon's most outstanding athlete. Other various plaques and trophies poured in, and I gave each one to my parents for safekeeping. They oohed and aaahed over every new honor. It was all happening so fast I didn't really know how to respond.

After the season ended I was cleaning out my locker as I retraced the year in my mind. My thoughts were cut short when Mouse sneaked up behind me and placed a hand around my waist.

"Can you believe it, kid?" he asked, pinching my side.

"Only you, Mouse," I smiled. "We showed 'em, huh?"

Mouse had never mentioned professional football as a possibility for me. In fact, he had avoided the issue, afraid to get my hopes up for some kind of pipe dream. Which is why his next words startled me.

"Kid, don't trust anybody," he warned. "Sometime soon we'll start finding you an agent. Right now, you just keep sight of what's important. Love your mommy and daddy, work hard in school, and remember, we play football for fun. The records are just gravy. You still got another year. Don't spoil it."

My eyes glittered with excitement. "Do you really think I've got a chance? I mean, the *NFL?*" I knew I was probably getting ahead of myself, but I had to ask.

Mouse was quiet for several seconds. This was as new to him as it was to me. All of his quarterbacks had experienced some degree of success with his system, but none had held a candle to the statistics I piled up.

"Neil," he finally said softly in a fatherlike tone of voice. "Don't jump to conclusions."

"But you're the best college quarterback I've ever seen."

I swallowed hard. I realized then what was riding on me. I had been dreaming for so long myself that I hadn't noticed that others were attaching their dreams to me, too: Mom, Dad, Stu, Valerie, Mitch . . . and maybe, to some degree, even Mouse. If I succeeded, they succeeded, too. If I failed, their hopes might be crushed. Mouse, who was an unorthodox coach at a little, "no-account" school, was riding my arm into the record books.

It was an awesome responsibility.

The summer before my senior year, every ring of the phone meant one of three things: my parents, a friend, or an agent. Agents were coming out of nowhere to offer me "deals I couldn't refuse." I heard more lies than a caddie on the thirteenth hole at Augusta.

"You're gonna be an easy first-round pick," they all promised. "Poor representation could be a million-dollar mistake." How true. Problem was, half of these guys looked like million-dollar mistakes. Mouse had already opened a two-inch-thick file on agents for me, and the information he had was incredible. Unlike many coaches, Mouse was very concerned with my future and became actively involved. He wanted me to avoid the pitfalls agents presented.

During the hunt for clients agents get down to the nitty-gritty. This is a dirty, nasty side of football few fans ever really see, or understand. The competition for recruits is slick and cutthroat, and guidelines become a matter of conscience, not law. It is quite common for agents to sign players while they are still in college, and easy for players still in college to accept money from agents. But Mouse wasn't buying. The pursuit for my services by scores of agents brought out a side of Mouse I had never seen before.

My middle-class Lake Oswego upbringing didn't prepare me to handle the first-class pressure put on me. Fortunately, with the help of my parents and Mouse, we steered clear of shady agents early on. Little did I know, however, that down the road all the attention from agents would become a thorn in the side. All but one.

Leigh Steinberg, a sports attorney from Berkeley, California, visited my family on August 2, 1980. I remember picking him up at the airport and driving him out to the house. He looked barely old enough to be thirty-one. Nearly six feet tall, with a slim, athletic build, he had a disconcerting, movie-star look about him. His striking blue eyes, black, curly hair, and golden tan flattered his clean-cut image and, coupled with his toothy smile and electric charm, made him appear almost too good to be true. Young, relaxed, with a big wad of tobacco in his mouth, he was as nonchalant as they come. A graduate of the University of California-Berkeley Law School, he lacked the arrogant aura you'd expect to go along with such credentials. "No pressure, Neil," he said in the car, as he leaned back and made himself at home. "You are the one who has to be comfortable in your career."

Leigh already represented Atlanta Falcons quarterback Steve Bartkowski. Leigh had met Bart as a grad counselor in the dorms at Cal. After graduating first in his class in 1974, Leigh spent some time touring the world. But by early 1975 he was considering becoming a Los Angeles district attorney, although he had received seventeen offers in corporate law.

At the same time, Bart's negotiations with the Atlanta Falcons as the first pick of the 1975 draft had come to a stalemate. So Steve fired his attorney and approached his old friend Leigh, who had never represented an athlete in his life. Out of friendship, Leigh accepted and instantly proved he was a natural. Although the now-defunct World Football League was on its last legs, Leigh started a bidding war for Bart between the WFL and the Falcons and wrangled Atlanta's offer up to more than double their previous bid. When Steve finally went with the Falcons, he signed the largest working contract in NFL history, and Leigh Steinberg's career was born.

My high regards for Steve—and June—were largely why I was so interested in Leigh. And the more I heard him talk that day in the car, the more I liked him. He never offered anything—no money, no cars, no jewelry, or clothes. Just a simple promise to do the best job he could do when the time came.

"Being a lawyer is a tool for me to help in the development of young men's lives," he said. "To develop a happy life in football, you must have a strong nucleus, such as your spiritual beliefs, and you must keep your priorities in order." Leigh used our time together to explore who I was and what I was about. He challenged me to think of the possibility of life without football. He spent painstaking, quality time discussing my career with my parents, who were more than eager to participate.

Two days later I flew to Seattle to watch the Seahawks and Atlanta Falcons play in an exhibition game. Meeting me there was Bill Moore, agent for Walsh and Associates and then-Seahawks quarterback Jim Zorn. I also spent some time with Steve Bartkowski and I was awed to be called his friend. Steve really was a role model for me after he became a Christian, and to this day I don't think he realizes what an impact he had on my life.

Needless to say, I was more than impressed . . . but also troubled. I felt the temptations in the fast life-style I was being introduced to. After the first night there, I was so moved by the wealth and power being thrown around I went back to my hotel room at the fancy Park Hilton in downtown Seattle and scribbled this note to my parents:

Dear Mom and Dad:

You know me fairly well, since I've grown up with you most of my life. You know I don't like to write letters or use a fancy sort of stationery to convey my messages. But I felt moved to write and share my feelings. For the first time, I realize what the term "wined and dined" means. What I've seen and heard so far about Walsh and Associates is very positive. I'm just not used to going first class, and I mean first class. I want to thank you for bringing me up to appreciate the hard and rough times in life. Not that it's murder living in Lake Oswego, but recently I've been experiencing and tasting (great steaks) the worldly part of life.

I don't know how to handle it. Please be in constant prayer for my actions and words. For God alone can lead me through this difficult and sometimes "strange" time in my career. I just want to say I love you both and I wish you could feel the love God is showing me now in a materialistic way. I know for a fact that you've both been a big part of my football and spiritual endeavors, and I thank you. But thanks be to God, who gives us the victory through Jesus Christ our Lord (1 Corinthians 15:57).

In Christ's Abundant Love,
Neil

By the fall of 1980, I was a year older, a year smarter, a year stronger, and I was ready to play a year better than my junior season. I was putting more pressure on myself than anyone else was to have a big year. I wasn't sure how tough the press or the public were going to be on me, but I knew that whatever happened, I would remain strong.

"Stay concerned with having fun playing football, and think about others, not yourself," Ron Kincaid continued to warn. "A senior should enjoy every game, and if you can't, it ruins the fun of it." I didn't want that to happen to me. I wanted to be more than just Neil Lomax. We were a team. And with Mouse, that would be the only way it would be; otherwise, as he would say, "Get your butt on down the road."

*   *   *

When we started practicing, more faces than usual began to pop up in the stands. Hardly a week passed that I wasn't under the scrutiny of one professional scout or another. It was a novelty at first, but by year's end I would be downright tired of the distraction.

September 8, 1980, finally rolled around, and we opened my final college season against North Dakota. On film they looked about as threatening as a cap gun, and on the field they weren't much better. We started slowly, however, so they made it a game for a while. By the second quarter, though, I knew their defensive backs were no match for our speedsters on the corners.

I was rolling to my right early in the second period, when I saw Stu just leave his man sitting still going down the sideline. I planted and cut the football loose. It spiraled, laces spinning, in a high arc over Stu's right shoulder. I hadn't put enough on it, and Stu had to slow down just a hair to make the catch, which gave the defender just enough time to get within arm's reach. Stu looked back over his shoulder, made a brilliant catch, and headed to the goal line. But in a last-gasp effort, the exhausted defensive back dove at Stu, and his upper body landed on Stu's right leg. Under the added weight of the defender, Stu's right foot stuck in the turf when he tried to pull away in a regular running motion.

His knee exploded. The ligaments tore away violently. Not realizing how serious the injury was, he courageously played into the second quarter. But by halftime, the pain overwhelmed him, and team doctors relayed the bad news.

"He's finished," Leo Marty, our trainer, told Mouse. "He's through for the year."

Stu was lying on the training table, right arm draped across his eyes. Most of his pads had been removed. His T-shirt, stained from sweat, drooped off his stomach. The right leg of his game pants had been rolled high above the swollen knee, where an ice pack was failing to provide temporary relief from the pain. I grabbed his left hand and squeezed. "Why?" Stu asked, his voice trembling and his breath coming in heaves. His grip tightened. "Why . . . why me?"

It made me sick to my stomach. I didn't have any answer. For

years coaches had warned us that "football is a game of violence
. . . it can all come to an end at any time." But never had I seen
such an up-close example. When it's your best friend on his back,
it hits close to home. This could be the end of not only his college
career, but also any hopes for the pros. For an instant, my mind
tormented me with thoughts like *What if that were me?* I pushed
them out of my mind as we went out to play the second half. We
won 28–14, but losing Stu bittered the usual sweetness of victory.
After Stu's injury, nobody really had his heart in the game.

After the game I visited Stu at his girl friend's apartment. The
crutches were leaning up against the sofa. Stu's pain had
changed. He was bitter, angry. "Why did it have to be me?" he
asked vehemently as his girl friend consoled him. I really didn't
know what to say to him. "What did I ever do to deserve this?
This is the thanks I get for trying to make something of myself.
Why?"

You could feel the fight, the will to overcome, bleeding out of
him. He was giving up on himself. Stu kept his date with the surgeon the next morning. I felt worse when I looked at Sunday's
Oregonian; the words tore at my guts:

> . . . Gaussoin suffered major ligament damage in the first half
> of the Portland State Vikings' 28–14 season-opening victory
> over North Dakota. Gaussoin, the nation's leading pass re-
> ceiver, will miss the remainder of the 1980 football season.

After being my most dependable receiver for seven years, Stu
had caught his last pass—ever—from me.

I fought back the tears.

By mid-season, we were 3–2, and Mouse was running us harder
than ever. After another long practice one week before the East
Washington game we filed into the locker room exhausted, helmets dangling in our hands. I was ready to drop as I walked up
the hard concrete steps into our locker room. Suddenly, a huge
black man, over six-five, approached me and stuck out his big
right hand.

"Hey there, son," he said. I couldn't believe this guy. From his ten-gallon hat to his tight-fitting blue jeans and snakeskin boots, he was clearly a Texan. I shook his hand, which was adorned with nickle-sized diamond rings.

"Good to meet ya, boy," he said gruffly, scratching his goatee. "I represent Jerry Argovitz." At that time, Argovitz was a very hot Texas sports agent whose big deals had made the media coast-to-coast—and raised some questions as well. "I'd like to have dinner with you," he continued. "I'm staying down at the Hilton; here's my card. I really don't want to bother you now, but we'll come by with a limousine in a little while."

He looked around, and noticing that he had attracted the attention of all my teammates, picked up the pitch. "Yeah, we'll be by in a big limo," he said, flashing a toothy grin. "You'll have one of the best dinners of your life, and Jerry's footing the bill. Jerry wants to get to know you. I'm only gonna be here a few days and I really want to get to know you, too."

I grabbed the bottom of my practice jersey and wiped sweat from my face, then forced a smile. "Thanks," I said. "But I don't really have the time to do something like that right now. We've got team meetings tonight. But thanks anyway." I turned to walk into the locker room, and his big hand grabbed my shoulder.

"Wait a minute, kid," he said. "I came all the way to Portland from Houston just to talk to you. I just wanna be nice to you."

I shook my head. "No thanks," I reiterated. He wouldn't let go. "You're making a mistake," he said, his voice getting louder.

The next thing I heard was loud cussing from the stairwell. Mouse, who had heard the last part of the conversation, knew what was transpiring and he roared to my defense.

"Hey, hey, hey," he snapped, his legs pumping hard to get him up the steps in a flash. Without batting an eye, Mouse looked a full two feet upward at the big agent.

"I'm Mouse Davis," he bellowed. "I'm the head coach here. I suggest you leave the big kid alone." The huge black guy just looked past him at me, but Mouse was on him again before he had time to speak. "You got something to say?" Mouse fired. "Say it to me."

I turned away again. "Yeah," I said. "Talk to my coach." But the agent stepped toward me and reached out; "Wait, Neil," he said. Like a striking snake, Mouse grabbed his thick arm. He wasn't playing around. The guy towered over him, but Mouse didn't blink; he had that look on his face that I've only seen a few times.

"I said leave the kid alone," Mouse spit between gritted teeth. "Don't make me tell you again."

The man backed up. "I'll talk to him later," he told Mouse. Mouse's eyes narrowed into slits.

"Like hell you will," he retorted. Argovitz's man started down the steps, leaving a string of obscenities in his wake. Mouse just stood at the top with his arms crossed. We never saw or heard from the guy again.

We whipped East Washington, 54–21, and I threw 4 touchdowns in less than two quarters of work, 2 to Clint Didier, who now plays tight end for the Redskins. The next week we prepared for Cal Poly-Pomona, which was coached by Roman Gabriel, the former quarterback of the Los Angeles Rams and my boyhood idol. In Pop Warner football I had worn number 18 because it was his number in the pros. I couldn't wait to meet him. Prior to the game we ran out to mid-field and chatted for a few minutes as he watched his team warm up.

"You've sure had a great career," he said, smiling. "Go easy on us tonight." I laughed. From the looks of it, he had a pretty solid club, and I figured I was in for a rough night.

Roman's team put together a long drive, but only managed a single touchdown. Meanwhile, we were unstoppable. Mouse barely let me play—every time I put the ball up we either scored or came close. Again, in less than two quarters, I threw for 339 yards and 3 touchdowns. If Mouse had let me go the distance, he said I could've thrown for 1,000 yards against these guys. It was that easy. Gabriel was furious. He watched the entire game tight-lipped, and by the second half he had quit yelling encouragement to his players. We won, 93–7.

Afterward, Roman didn't even speak. A few days later he told the Associated Press that Mouse had played me for the entire game just to make a statement, to make it clear that I should be a first-round draft pick. I hadn't even played a total of two quarters. He also accused Mouse of purposely running up the score. That was never the case. Mouse played his second and third string, but with the offense, it made no difference. It was the offense, not always just the players, that kept the ball rolling.

When Mouse heard about it, he just shrugged.

"Next time we play 'em," Mouse grinned, "we'll start the cheerleaders—and still win." Maybe it didn't bother him, but my boyhood idol had disappointed me.

Early the next week, my phone rang. It was my mother, and she couldn't mask her excitement. The *Los Angeles Times* had featured me in a wire story. She read me parts of it over the phone:

> "I'll tell you what, the guy is a lot better than I thought he was," Gil Brandt, director of personnel for the Dallas Cowboys, said.
>
> ". . . the guy reminds me, in terms of arm strength and leadership ability, of Roger Staubach.
>
> "He's definitely a first-round draft choice. When he gets drafted, a lot of guys will wonder what this quarterback from Portland State is doing being drafted so high.
>
> "They won't wonder after they see him play."

Wow. Gil Brandt. The Dallas Cowboys. My boyhood dream was to be on a team like the Cowboys, and I began to realize I was only months away from such an opportunity. All year long I had been staying late after practice to run and throw for scouts. I remembered the Dallas scout and how hard I had worked for him. To be a first-round draft choice is the ultimate recognition of athletic ability. I hardly dared hope it would happen to me.

One of the most painful moments of the year, after Stu's injury, was when fullback Joel Sigel went down with a cracked bone in his foot. Joel was a workhorse, one of those solid, give-everything players. He hated going in to tell Mouse he couldn't play. Mouse did that to you. You wanted to play for him so bad, that when you physically couldn't, it actually hurt inside.

Joel said he sat down with Mouse and muttered a few words about not being able to play the rest of the year. "Mouse hardly said a word," Joel mumbled later. "He just looked at me softly, with those eyes, like, 'I understand.' Finally, he said, 'Hang in there, kid.' We both had watery eyes."

So we prepared for Delaware State without our starting fullback, and Mouse was concerned. "On paper, these kids look pretty doggone tough," Mouse told me a few days before the game. "We may have made a mistake scheduling these guys."

In the first quarter of the game, we had the ball 3 minutes and 57 seconds total. With 1:02 remaining in the first quarter, Mouse took me out of the game. I had completed twelve of eighteen passes for 254 yards and 7 touchdowns. *In one quarter.* Three times we scored on long passes on first down, as I threw touchdowns to virtually every receiver we had. On the sidelines, we weren't even celebrating. It was almost embarrassing. We were giving one another looks like, "Can you believe this?" They weren't that bad a team, but they just weren't prepared to play the kind of pass defense it took to hold us down.

We went up 42–0 and were preparing to kick off when Mouse turned to me. "Put your jacket on," he ordered. "You're coming out. I'm gonna let some of the other kids play the second quarter." Well, they fumbled the kickoff, and I looked at Mouse.

"Hey," I said, "it's still the first quarter. Let me get one more." Mouse smiled, "Okay. Let's try Rip Scramble Left Spit End. Put one in there for the scouts."

I rolled left as my receivers blanketed out all over the field. The strong safety hesitated just for a second as Kenny Johnson ran past him, and I whipped it loose. Kenny went 27 yards for the score. I nonchalantly walked off the field. Mouse slapped me on the butt. "That was one for the training reel, baby," he yelled.

Delaware State was literally shell-shocked. Their defensive players had no idea what they should do. They were hollering around to each other in mass confusion. I tallied 8 touchdowns total on the night, and we won 105–0 in a college single-game scoring record that still stands. I ran my string of touchdowns to 98, breaking Doug Williams record of 93.

And I still had two games to play.

By now, the crush of attention I was a getting was threatening to engulf me and my family. Not a day went by that either agents or scouts weren't calling, visiting my parents, or watching practice. Mouse shielded me when he could, but my parents were exposed to all of it, and the sudden attention was getting to them. Being a Christian was a big help for me. In this situation, you either sink or swim. If you start thinking you're big stuff, you will lose all your friends and isolate yourself from people you love. The attention I got did cause waves. I tried to be sensitive to what people thought about me, but it was hard to be just one of the guys.

While I did my best to ignore the publicity, my parents were enjoying it immensely. They were so proud of my achievements that it seemed to become the focal point of their lives. Jokingly, Terry had T-shirts made for them with *Neil Lomax for Heisman* printed on the front. To them, it was no joke. They wore those T-shirts until they were threadbare. Every week they attended the PSU booster luncheon, which honored the player of the week. Most often, I was the player of the week, and my parents would end up basking in the glow and proudly saying what a great son I was. They had become "Neil Lomax's parents," kind of celebrities themselves. Nothing made my dad's day more fulfilling than for one of his co-workers to say, "Hey, your boy's doing pretty well." Then Dad would bore him with all the facts from my latest outing.

With my parents, friends, and classmates all wanting to talk about how big my name was getting, it was Ron Kincaid, again, who helped me keep things in perspective. During one visit at the church, we sat in his office and just talked. It wasn't counseling, it was merely friendship. I was maturing, and Ron recognized my growth.

"Neil, you have a good understanding of God and who He is," Ron said. "You are struggling with all this publicity, but if you realize God is great, and how small we are, you'll keep everything in perspective. All your success is God-given. And all your records don't mean anything when compared to God. Don't ever lose your devotion to God or quit obeying Him. God could take the fame instantly. Just as fast as it came upon you."

I nodded. It made me think of Stu. "Well, Ron," I answered. "If things don't work out with football, people have been telling me I've got a good face for radio."

We both laughed.

But all the attention did get to me in curious ways sometimes. Once, on a typical Portland day on which a steady rainstorm had colored the city an ugly, overcast gray, I walked down the sidewalk to a little house on Twenty-ninth Street that I shared with teammates John Kincheloe and Joel Fredericks. The mountains weren't even visible in the haze. My shoulders shivered under my thin jacket as I carried a sackful of groceries under my arm.

That's when I noticed him.

Leaning against a tree about twenty yards way was a man in a gray London Fog-type trenchcoat, his ominous eyes peering out from under a cheap, low-cut gray fedora. I glanced around nervously, and a quick look down the street behind me confirmed my thoughts: I was alone. I turned up the walk to the house when I heard his heels clicking on the sidewalk.

Oh, God, I thought. *This is it. I've read about stuff like this.*

I walked faster. So did he. For nearly eight years I had relied on my ability to think fast on the football field. Yet now, my mind was blanker than a tubeless television. *I guess if I dropped the groceries, I could take him,* I thought. *But I've got eggs in here!*

The man was right behind me. I wheeled to face him, but hung on to my groceries.

"Neil Lomax?" he rasped eerily. By now, I was thoroughly spooked and ready for anything.

"Yeah," I said as gruffly as I could manage.

"I need to talk to you," he said. His eyes stared at me coldly as he reached inside his coat.

"Oh, no," I sighed, expecting to see the steely gleam of a nickle-plated .357 Magnum.

"What?" he asked, pulling a portfolio from his pocket. I breathed a sigh of relief.

"Who are you?" I demanded.

"Well, I've represented some people and I'd like to represent you." He nervously held out the portfolio, his hand fidgeting. I leaned away as if it were spoiled milk.

"Sir, I've been hounded by people trying to represent me. Thanks, but no thanks."

"But you don't understand what I've gone through to find you. That coach of yours—the Mouse guy—gave me the wrong address. He had me traipsing all over the other side of town."

I held back a smile. I could see Mouse roaring with laughter at the thought of a would-be agent going door to door on foot looking for me.

I shook my head at the agent, walked inside the house, and locked the door. My heart was still pounding, and I leaned against the door for several seconds. It startled me when he banged loudly on the door, and I leaped away.

"Pleeeez," he yelled. "Just talk with me for a minute. I can get you money, cars, whatever you want."

"Oh, Lord," I muttered to myself, rolling my eyes. I pulled the blinds, but peeked out from one side. He stood in the yard for at least thirty minutes before he finally stomped away in disgust.

I fell back into a chair and let out a long breath. Thank goodness I hadn't wasted my entire week's groceries on him.

In our next-to-last game on November 15, 1980, I threw 3 more touchdowns to help beat South Dakota State 48–17. That week, things started happening left and right. First, I was flown to Dallas to accept the Fellowship of Christian Athletes Player of the Year Award. No sooner did I return than I was publicly an-

nounced as a quarterback in the East-West Shrine Game in Palo
Alto, California, on January 10. I couldn't believe it. Me, from
tiny PSU, would get to play with the best college talent in the
country. I was speechless when I heard the news, and just a little
jittery. Leigh Steinberg, who I had nearly decided would be my
choice to be my attorney, wrote my parents a letter:

Dear Mr. and Mrs. Lomax:

*Well your baby has hit the coast-to-coast news services. How
can someone be a "sleeper" in the draft after nationwide television and newspaper coverage? If you need a place to stay for the
Shrine game, I have plenty of room at my Berkeley house.*

Leigh

That meant a lot to me. A lot of agents had promised me the
world, but none had invited my parents to stay in their home. In
the meantime, a runner for agent Mike Trope came to see me.
Trope represented Earl Campbell and several other name players,
and his runner offered me a car and wanted to take me to dinner.
By this time, I was really getting sick of the whole charade.
Trope's reputation went all the way back to his college days,
where it was reported that he was involved in fixing student government elections. At age twenty he became an agent, and his
aggressive activities forced him to hire a bodyguard. His first cli-
ent was Johnny Rodgers, the 1972 Heisman Trophy winner from
Nebraska. Then he signed Anthony Davis of USC. His whole
hustle was to sign big-name athletes early, get them high-salary,
big-bonus contracts, and defer most of the money. The size of the
"million-dollar" contracts made great newspaper copy, but the
athletes were left with little cash up front and years of deferred,
interest-free money that depreciated through inflation.

"These are the type of contracts top draft picks are getting,"
Leigh warned me. "They are getting a big pop up front, a huge
bonus deferred out a long way. The salaries are proportioned in
increments like $50,000 each year for five years. Why does an
agent choose a contract like that? Because he can get more

money for himself if he's taking a percentage of the bonus up front.

"With a $600,000 bonus, the agent can get $60,000 right now," Leigh explained. "Actually, by taking a percentage of the contract up front, the agent is making more than the percentage he contracted for. What is reported in the papers as a million-dollar contract is, in real dollars, $500,000 or less, when all the deferred salary is accurately measured. Yet the agent takes his percentage off the $1-million face value."

It's no wonder the agent business is so hot, and Leigh's honesty meant everything. Although I didn't understand all he was telling me, Mouse did, and he liked Leigh's approach very much. Furthermore, what Leigh said was supported in the papers. When Mike Trope signed Earl Campbell, he said he got him "over a million bucks." But the money was deferred for forty years, interest-free. Leigh said his fee would be up to me. "You, Neil, determine how much I should be paid," he said. To me, that said it all about Leigh Steinberg.

In the midst of all the recruitment hoopla, I still had one game to play. Our final game, at home, was against Big Sky opponent Weber State. Mouse looked tired. We were 7–3, and it had been a long year. A happy one, but long. Mouse had virtually lived at the school and was constantly preparing for games, making speeches, fighting off hungry agents, giving game film to scouts, or spending time with his players. The man had given every ounce of energy he had to a football program which, the year before he came, had been one of the worst in the country. As we dressed for this game, we were riding atop the highest publicity wave ever given to a I-AA school. His club had done more offensively than any other in history, at any level.

It was a somber moment, putting on that green jersey for the last time. There wasn't a lot of conversation in the locker room when Mouse stepped forward.

"It's been a good year," he said, rubbing his face. "God knows I've loved you kids. But if we don't win tonight, they're gonna remember you as losers. If we win tonight, you guys have a shot at the play-offs, maybe even a national championship. You're only as good as your last game." He turned and walked away. He didn't have to say anything else. I wanted to win so bad for Mouse and the team I couldn't wait to get on the field.

We were sky-high at kickoff. The old electricity in the air, which we felt when we knew we were going to dominate, was there. So was Terry, in the giant Mouse outfit, dancing and jestering for the last time that year.

From the opening play, I was hot, and we inflicted a beating on Weber State like they hadn't gotten in four years of playing us. Every pass I threw, it was like I had seen it before. Since it was the last game of the year, Mouse left me in longer than normal, and I wasn't letting him down. We controlled them. Finally, early in the fourth quarter and with us winning 50–0, he called me aside.

"Big kid, this is it. Complete one more pass, and we're gonna pull you out and let the crowd give you a standing ovation, and you can throw them a kiss or whatever you want to do," Mouse said. He didn't look at me. It was an emotional moment for both of us.

I ran back in and called a quick pass to wide receiver Clint Didier and hit him on the numbers. But the defensive back fell down, and Clint went the distance for the touchdown and the whole team came off the field. Mouse called me over again. "As soon as you complete another short pass, you're coming out," he repeated.

Our next possession, I looked for Dave Semantel on a short little out-pattern. This would surely get me out of the game, I thought. But Dave turned his defensive back around and I laid it up top; he made the catch and scored from nearly 80 yards out. By now I was laughing when I walked to the sideline. Mouse was smiling, but wouldn't look my way.

Weber fumbled the kickoff, and now we had first-and-goal

from like the 2-yard line. Mouse had already taken all his seniors but me out of the game and it was getting late.

"Neil, do not throw the ball," he said as I snapped my helmet and trotted on. "Run the ball," he yelled behind me.

I called a fullback dive play in the huddle. When I took the snap, a hole opened up in the line big enough to walk through. It would be an easy touchdown. But instead of making the handoff properly, I waited and waited until the fullback was almost past me. At the last second, I shoveled the ball into his stomach. He almost dropped it, and instantly, the defense was on him for a loss.

Mouse waved me off. The crowd stood and roared. Four years: 13,220 yards passing; 106 touchdowns; twelve 400-yard games; twenty-eight 300-yard games; 938 completions.

All NCAA records. For all divisions. Not to mention the ninety division I-AA records I had stacked up.

The final score was 75–0. As we were running off the field, the Weber State coach yelled at Mouse, "You couldn't beat us like that without that Lomax kid."

"Yep," Mouse answered. "And we got Lomax. We're not ashamed of that."

"Not anymore," the coach fired back.

The smile slowly disappeared from Mouse's face.

He idled up to me as I was getting dressed and slapped my arm.

"As far as execution, I've never seen a quarterback play better than you just did. They'd blitz, you'd recover and lay it up top for a touchdown. They'd play zone, you'd find the seam. They'd cover your primary receiver, you'd find the secondary receiver.

"You really gave the scouts something to take home."

Mouse hugged me.

In the corner of the room sat Stuart, quietly taking in the scene. His bad leg was propped on the bench in front of him.

6

The First Round

"... no matter how thorough the planning, how shrewd the forecasts, nobody could say for certain how the draft would unfurl. (The scouts) would be prepared for their task, but draft day action is a deck that won't be stacked. Invariably, they end up playing the hands they are dealt."

—Steve Cassady,
The Selection Process

"Next."

The doctor's voice rang out over the high school gymnasium. Like a herd of cattle, the line of fifty or more of the best college football players moved forward for their physicals during talent evaluations "combines" from various NFL scouts and player personnel. Just days away from several "all-star" bowl games, I felt like a biology experiment as I paraded around before hundreds of scouts. In my undershorts, no less. It was like a beauty pageant. You had to walk down a ramplike platform, announce your name, height, weight, and position, and walk back. The scouts and doctors looked on carefully, scribbled on their charts, and watched some more.

I had decided on Leigh Steinberg as my attorney, though our agreement at the time was just a handshake at the airport. Although I had been picked for the Japan Bowl and Blue-Gray game, too, he suggested I play in the East-West game and the Senior Bowl in Mobile, Alabama. When I arrived in Palo Alto, California, I couldn't believe the first-class show to which we were treated. First they took us all south to Los Angeles, Disneyland, then the Rose Bowl Game, and finally to San Francisco for a week of practice.

Many players had yet to make a decision on an agent. Therefore, the hotel was teeming with agents. There were more agents checked into the hotel than players, fans, or coaches. My roommate was David Verser, a black wide receiver from Kansas, and things got so bad we had to quit answering our phone. Every time we stepped out into the hall we were mobbed by agents. Chuck Dekaedo, an agent in the early seventies, once recalled the "sinister" recruiting efforts of agents in Palo Alto. "The agents were straight out," he says. "They would ask a kid, 'Hey, you want a girl? I've got a girl stashed here.' And they would grease palms with money."

By the time I was there, such efforts had intensified. It was like a meat market. We would return from practice, and ten business cards had been shoved under our door. One guy was incredibly persistent. A short, beady-eyed man with a stomach protruding over his belt, he stopped me in the lobby. It was obvious from his sales pitch that he had read articles about my faith and beliefs.

"Hey, Neil," he said, his lips flapping like a flag in the wind. "Family is real important to me, too. Religion, in fact, is a big part of my life. It's important to me that you find somebody who can help you keep these things important in your life. You need to have help setting up a budget, working things out for tax purposes, handling charities, and you know, all the other things."

He wiped his brow, which was wet from perspiration. *This guy is either slick or sick,* I thought. *If he's telling the truth, maybe he isn't such a bad guy.* But a few hours later I came back into the hotel, and the codger had cornered David Verser. As I strolled past, I overheard him giving David an entirely different story, but in his same rapid-fire fashion.

"First, man, we gotta get you a brand-new car," he said. "Then, buy your folks a house; you gotta take care of your folks, you know." He reached out and patted David's shirt. "Hey, *brother,* clothes are important to me, too," he continued, again wiping the ever-present sweat that beaded on his forehead. "Jewelry, man, all the jewelry you want, man. You gotta set yourself up and make sure you make the right impression on people. David, the main thing with our association is to make sure you, David Verser, are set up with everything you want, and that you are happy in your pro career."

He left out the part, however, about where he gets 10 percent of your earnings, which would've gone a long way toward buying more clean hankies to wipe off all that nervous sweat of his. I walked up in the middle of his spiel, and the guy nearly swallowed his tongue when he saw me. He thrust a business card into David's pocket. "I'll call you," he said, scampering off.

Despite all the little annoyances, the week proved to be the start of a valuable friendship with Arizona State wide receiver John Mistler. We had identical personalities, and we hit it off in our first practice session for the West team. He was the kind of player who would come out early for practice and stay late afterward to glean out every bit of ability he could muster. We had some great times that week in the Bay area. Some not so great too. It was a new experience to be propositioned in Chinatown by two "ladies of the night." One told John, "It'll cost you a hundred bucks for a good time, sugar." John looked at her in mock disbelief. "A good time?" he asked. "I had a good time at Disneyland and it didn't cost me anything!"

All the distractions took their toll on the field. The first problem was the crowd; I had never played before eighty thousand people in my life. Most of my teammates were from schools like Nebraska, USC, Oklahoma, and so on, so they didn't pay any mind to the huge throng of people. I, on the other hand, stood for several minutes after we took the field and just stared around, panning from one end of the stadium to the other, in awe of the buzzing mass of fans. That was the highlight of the afternoon. I was worried to death about whether my tiny school experience would measure up to these hulking all-Americans. But I was very proud to be representing "tiny" Portland State.

Maybe it was fear, or just a lack of confidence, but I played horribly. I tried to force a few balls to John, but the timing simply wasn't there. We got drilled, 21–3, and I was relieved to get out of there.

Mobile was also packed with coaches, agents, and scouts, but it was quite a different story when we assembled for the thirty-second Senior Bowl Game. The only thing there was to do in Mobile was play football, and they had our complete attention from the first day we arrived.

The staff of the San Francisco 49ers coached our team, and I was quickly realizing what a business football really was. Bill Walsh, the 49ers' head coach, pulled no punches about the seriousness of the occasion.

"Gentlemen, you're here on a business trip," he said. "We have business to conduct and business will conclude on Saturday after the game. We're here for one reason, we're all getting paid to conduct business, and if you're not here for business you may as well leave right now."

I spent most of the week in my room, and I studied hard. My poor performance in the East-West Game could really hurt my chances in the draft if I followed it with another bad game here. Each night, I flipped through the playbook they had given us and 49ers offensive coordinator Sam Wyche came to my room to tutor me. The night before the game, though, I caught myself looking at pictures of past Most Valuable Players, which included Steve Bartkowski. Staring at the ceiling later that night, I was lost in my thoughts. Here I was, traveling all over the country, playing on national television and in front of millions of people. I imagined myself in my Senior Bowl uniform, completing pass after pass, the roar of the crowd in my ears. Portland suddenly seemed so far away.

"Lord," I prayed before falling asleep, "I honestly thank You for the way You've seen fit to bless me. Help me find a way to handle my success. Show me, please, how to continue to serve You. And Lord, help me tomorrow. I'm gonna need it."

They told us we were in the deep South, but the cold tailwind that blistered my ears through my helmet on game day sure didn't remind me of what I'd heard of Dixie. But I warmed things up quickly on the field. *These guys are no better than you,* I told myself. I refused to doubt my ability just because I wasn't from a big school. Sticking to the fundamentals Mouse had drilled into me for four years, I put on a passing clinic. I scrambled away from the huge defensive linemen from Pitt and Penn State. I put pinpoint passes just out of reach of the great defensive backs from Alabama and Auburn. In less than two quarters of play, in a typical, drop-back style offense, I threw for 167 yards as we won 23–10.

Just before the game ended, a special announcement filtered down the sideline. "Hey, Lomax," Coach Wyche yelled. "I think they named you the MVP." I couldn't believe it. Sure enough, I was greeted in the locker room afterward by CBS announcers Curt Gowdy and Dick Stockton, and later game officials awarded me with a gorgeous trophy.

Back home in Portland, my mom was only too happy to shine it up and add it to her rapidly growing collection in the living room.

Spring was exhausting. There are four or five scouting combines in the NFL, and every team but the Los Angeles Raiders belongs to one. So instead of every team having to evaluate you individually, one scouting organization provides information to eight or nine teams. Shortly after my senior season ended, the combines began flying me all over the country, and scouts and doctors tested me for every imaginable physical strength and weakness.

The first complaint that came up concerned my feet. Doctors said my ankles were pronated. My feet are flat, and the bone structure around my ankles is really unusual. When passing, as I push off my back foot, my ankle tends to "roll over" the top of my shoe. Just from looking, it appears as if I'm bowlegged, but that's not really the case. But I had played four years on artificial turf at Portland State and my feet had never been an issue. I had never been blazing fast, but the condition wasn't a source of pain. But doctors wrote down on scouting reports that "it could be a problem on artificial turf." The Green Bay Packers sent me to a specialist, and he decided that "years of pounding on turf could take their toll." What they meant was that I didn't pass their physical. *So I got ugly feet; what does that have to do with throwing a football?* I thought.

I checked out healthy on every other point. Personnel people from every team were on hand at one time or another, and the tests they put you through are really fascinating, but some border on stupidity. For instance, the Cowboys were very concerned with how far I could broad jump and vertical jump. To me, tests like that were a joke. "Jeez," Mouse always said. "If the kid can throw the ball and put it on the money, I don't care if he can't jump off his porch. It's football, not the Olympics."

Other tests included rapid eye reactions, muscle reactions to certain stimuli, and various running and throwing tests. And I ran the 40 more times than I care to remember. There were certain teams I had no interest in playing for, and when I knew their scouts or personnel people were looking on, I would intentionally loaf.

It was an exciting time, visiting all the different cities and meeting all the great players. The only drawback was missing most of my winter term at PSU, which prevented me from graduating in four years.

*   *   *

The selection process takes place in New York, where Pete Rozelle, NFL commissioner, leads the grand party. As many as four representatives from each team occupy the twenty-eight tables; each team has fifteen minutes to decide their pick, though most take less. When a decision is reached, the player's name is written on a three-by-five-inch card and delivered to Rozelle. Rozelle then takes the podium and makes the announcement: "John Doe has been selected by the Philadelphia Eagles." Loud murmuring is then heard as the pick is relayed via telephone to team headquarters.

Behind every high draft selection is a long, drawn-out process which few fans understand. Hours of watching game film, weeks of following college seniors around, and months of tracking college careers are just part of every decision. Questions abound: Did he improve constantly as a collegian? Does he have good work habits? Good background? Drug or attitude problems? Health problems? Can he play hurt? Is he a leader? How good was his competition?

It just begins there. It's impossible to really understand the intangibles that make a player a great professional. Countless collegian all-Americans couldn't cut the pro ranks; likewise, many superstar professionals, such as the Dolphins' Mark Clayton, didn't even start in college. Scouts are paid to project how a college kid may mature, and whether his raw talent could blossom into "impact" ability as a professional.

All teams break down their needs for the draft. When their turn comes up, they evaluate all existing talent, then either take the best player available or draft for need. For instance, a team may need offensive linemen, but if a "sure-pick" quarterback or running back is available, they may wait on a lineman and take a skill player.

The happenings behind closed doors on draft day are fascinating. Each club has a "war room," or the room where scouts and front-office brass assemble during the eighteen-hour draft day, in

their administrative offices. By 6:00 A.M. the room is packed full
with the general manager, director of player personnel, the
coaching staff, team doctors, surgeons, trainers, and secretaries.

On one wall is a board that extends twenty feet wide and from
the floor to the ceiling. Across the top are rating numbers, from
the lowest draftable score, 4.0, to the highest, usually a 10.0. Up
and down the borders, players are classified by position: quarterbacks, running backs, offensive linemen, and so on. Under the
horizontal headings, rectangular cards are attached magnetically,
each with a player's name written in bold, block letters. Underneath the letters are height, weight, time in the 40-yard dash, and
general rating score. As players are chosen, the cards are taken
down and placed on boards elsewhere in the room, under the
headings of the teams that drafted them.

On another wall is a list of over seven hundred players considered not good enough to waste a draft pick on. These players are
the ones who can be signed as free agents. No college senior is
overlooked on this board.

A line of communication is manned constantly with team representatives at the draft in New York, who banter relentlessly
about which team might pick which player next. Draft picks are
filtered from the person on the phone around the table. After a
player is picked, another name is mentioned. Coaches shout out
their preferences. Scouts stare at computer printouts and player
profiles. Executives sort through stacks of scouting reports. Doctors are questioned about injuries that may affect a kid's pro
career. For each round, a consensus is reached regarding the best
players still available who most suit the needs of the team. When
it appears certain a player will be picked, a team assistant calls
him to inform him he is about to be taken. Teams have been
known to make last-second changes, however, and the kid cele-
brates, only to find the team took somebody else.

Every year the future of thousands of young football collegians
rests on this system.

* * *

The week before the draft *Sports Illustrated* predicted I would "most assuredly" go in the first round, as did every other publication I read. I was wearing the attention well; in fact, I *knew* I was going to be a first-round pick and my quotes reflected my confidence. "Yeah," I told *Sports Illustrated*, "I'm hoping for somewhere on the West Coast, but it might be St. Louis or New York." Secretly, I was thinking the Rams or Denver, where the scouts had really seemed high on my talent.

"A lot of questions will be answered in just a few moments as this year's NFL draft gets underway, right here on ESPN."

April 28, 1981. The voice of announcer Jim Simpson carried through the living room of John Kincheloe's parents' house. We didn't have cable TV, so we went to their house to watch the draft. Staring from a recliner five feet away, I wiped sleep from my eyes; it was 7:00 A.M. on the West Coast. My parents sat on the sofa with John; other friends and relatives were gathered on the floor. I expected Stu to be there, but he wasn't. Several local television crews and reporters leaned against the wall patiently, waiting for that moment when they could capture the jubilance expressed when local boy Neil Lomax went in the first round of the National Football League draft.

"And the first pick of the draft is South Carolina's George Rogers, chosen by the New Orleans Saints."

My big moment had arrived. Any second now, I told myself, as I watched the draft proceedings on ESPN, oblivious to what was taking place in the twenty-eight "war rooms" around the league. More than an hour elapsed, and they were through about the first ten picks. With every pick, my mind rationalized why each team might want me. "And the New York Giants . . ." My racing mind interrupted: *Phil Simms hasn't been too healthy*, I thought. ". . . take linebacker Lawrence Taylor from North Carolina." My heart rose and fell with every name.

"And the Dallas Cowboys pick . . ." I held my breath. Gil Brandt had told everybody in the country what a hot prospect I was. The Cowboys took a defensive player. Both my parents groaned out loud. A reporter sat back and let out a deep sigh. My embarrassment was evident in my flushed cheeks. I put my head in my hands. I quit watching, but I couldn't help but listen. The first round ended.

"But the agents said you were a first-round pick," my mom whined, obviously wounded. She emphatically crossed her arms. "And can you believe the gall of that Gil Brandt?"

I smirked. The Cowboys' public relations machine had done it again. Dallas really overdoes the backslapping before the draft, kissing up to young players just in case it drafts them. I had been dumb enough to fall for it. I'd been so caught up in how men appraised me that I'd forgotten about the One who appraises us all. The first round had become very important to me. I felt ashamed. I had listened to the scouts, the reporters, and the agents, despite being warned by Ron Kincaid countless times. "Put your faith in man," he had said, "and man will let you down every time. Don't say you are or aren't going to do anything. You say you're gonna follow the Lord's will."

One, two, three picks elapsed in the second round. The elation, the cheering, the joking had turned into dead silence. Nobody was saying anything.

Finally, a jangling phone split the stillness.

I leaped from my chair and grabbed it off the wall. "Yeah," I said, panting. The caller was Joel Frank, a newscaster with KYXI, "1500 on your dial," and he greeted me with baffling news.

"What are your feelings about being drafted by the St. Louis Cardinals?" he asked. I was stunned.

"I haven't been . . ." my voice tailed off as I looked at the television.

"And the St. Louis Cardinals have taken Portland State quarterback Neil Lomax with the fourth pick of the second round," Jim Simpson was saying.

"Neil?" probed Joel. "Neil?"

"Uh, yeah, Joel," I stammered. "Uh, this is great. It's a great feeling to be a St. Louis Cardinal. I'm looking forward to playing for them."

All the media people had flicked on their cameras and were yelling questions. The house had gone from utter stillness to pandemonium. My parents were hugging each other. My friends high-fived me. I grabbed my coat.

"Gotta go," I said, knowing I needed to get home and call Leigh. I raced home with carloads of newspeople in tow. I ran in the house and called Leigh.

"Leigh, can you believe it?" I asked.

"Neil, I warned you there might be a chance you wouldn't go in the first round," he said. After quickly filling me in on the Cardinals, he told me to improve my attitude.

"Emphasize the positive," he said. "We'll sort out what happens later on. It's still a great honor. Put on a happy face. These things are a test of character. I'll be in touch. Just keep smiling and keep telling the media you can't wait to play for St. Louis."

I hung up the receiver. Instantly, the phone rang.

"Neil? This is Larry Wilson, the director of player personnel with the St. Louis Cardinals. Welcome to the Cardinals and the National Football League."

Thoughts were racing through my mind at one hundred mph. Leigh had warned that the St. Louis organization was "cheap" to its players, and cited its current payroll as proof. One of my former PSU teammates, wide receiver Dave Stief, was playing for the Cards, and his description of the tight management certainly didn't impress me any. But what affected me most was that they were not contenders. It was both a burden and an opportunity.

But beggars can't be choosers, and after the draft ordeal I was thankful.

"Glad to be a part of the team," I told Larry.

"We have big hopes for you," he said.

"See you soon."

I replaced the receiver. Glancing in a mirror, I imagined myself dropping back to throw against the Cowboys, as I instantly went from loving them to hating them. "Neil Lomax, the rookie sensation," I said, letting the words ring in my ears. I casually completed a long imaginary touchdown to win the game. The crowd went berserk in my mind, just as it had years ago in my backyard in Lake Oswego.

It was a dream come true.

7

The Dotted Line

"Contract negotiations were honorless, distasteful, and totally frightening experiences. There were no fixed rules and behavior varied radically, depending on the individuals involved. . . . I had expected to be refused, but there was a note of disrespect I hadn't anticipated."

—Pete Gent, *North Dallas Forty*

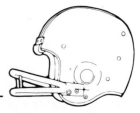

It was early May 1981, and the numbers that had been tossed around the war room during April's draft—"big kid, six-five, 270"—were coming to life. Real-life rookies were filing into a downtown St. Louis hotel the night before the first mini-camp of their lives. Until now we hadn't been people; we were merely numbers, grainy faces on black-and-white game film, the superstars of college press guides. Tomorrow, however, we would get our first chance to show our coaches they didn't make a mistake.

There was an air of optimism about the rookies. "This ain't that different from school," muttered a fourth-rounder, trying to appear acclimated. I was certainly out of my element, and it was hard to mask my excitement about actually being a part of a professional team. Rookies engage in a lot of nervous chatter, clearly thrilled to be where they are but tentative about what to do next.

In contrast to the rookies were the quiet free agents on hand— repeaters. These were guys who refused to let go of their dream of playing in the NFL; guys who were hanging on to every chance, knowing, but not admitting, that this might be their last one. Ricky Williams, a running back who had been cut by another team, had been through this process before. He stood off to the side, silently watching the proceedings.

Larry Wilson, director of player personnel, was inside the lobby shaking hands as each carload of new players arrived. "There's the guy they took in the first round," someone mumbled. E. J. Junior, a six-foot-three, 235-pound, all-American linebacker from the University of Alabama, unfolded from the automobile. All heads turned. He was big, and only a T-shirt covered his upper torso. "Little cold, huh?" asked Larry. "Not in Alabama," Junior grunted in his best Southern drawl. I smiled.

The assistant trainer, Jim "the Machine" Shearer, continued to introduce himself as newcomers came in shifts. "Check in and get your stuff to your room," he was saying, over and over. "Then fill out the information for your physical."

I noticed Stump Mitchell, a barrel-chested, ninth-round pick and a long shot to make the team. Great explosion off the ball, but only five-feet-nine-inches tall and not even 190 pounds.

"What do they want?" he asked.

"You need to fill out your physical information booklet," the trainer said, hustling over. Stump moved away. "How many times do I have to do this stuff?" the fireplug running back wondered aloud, asking a question the rest of us were all dying to ask ourselves.

"The doc will need it," the trainer replied. The hotel was

buzzing with young men as we looked over questionnaires on medical, public relations, and personal information.

E. J. walked into the room.

"Big dude," said James Mallard, a tenth-round hopeful wide receiver who had been a teammate of Junior's at Alabama. Everyone stared at E. J. The first-round pick got all the attention. I swallowed my pride as the others continued to appraise him. *I could've been him*, I thought. Ron Kincaid's advice rang in my mind . . . "be thankful in all things." I bit my lip and turned away, but Mallard kept talking.

"You should see him hit," he said. "Takes two or three guys to keep him out of the play."

"You ever blocked him in practice?" Stump asked.

"I sure tried," the kid answered.

The group laughed. Nervously.

Rudy Feldman, a graying, trim linebacker coach with a voice raspy from yelling, pushed his way into the room. He had already introduced himself to Junior; the coach *knew* E. J. could play. Instead, he was looking for Dave Ahrens, a risky, sixth-round draft pick out of Wisconsin who, according to Feldman, had his best football ahead of him. Against the wishes of some of the scouts, but because of Feldman's gut feeling, the kid was drafted.

He slapped Ahrens on the back. "You sure look good," Feldman said, his eyes scrolling carefully over the six-three, 247-pound linebacker. "You're gonna have to bust it in camp," he continued. Ahrens nodded. He *looked* hungry. If Feldman would've asked, Dave might've rammed his head through the wall right then, just to prove his desire. That's the kind of guy Dave was.

Feldman smiled. He had made a good decision, and his gut was telling him so; his confidence was reinforced by his up-close inspection of Ahrens.

Meanwhile, I was getting to know a few of the players around me. Every guy had a story to tell. There was Jeff Griffin, the third-round choice from Utah, Steve Rhodes, a fifth-round pick from Oklahoma, and John Gillen, a linebacker from Illinois. Cautiously I poked and parried in conversation, testing my words, not wanting to say anything stupid. I was so impressed with the first-class treatment, at least compared with my Portland State days, that I was quickly learning to like "the pros."

"It must be horrible to be treated so great and then get cut," I thought aloud. "Being cut, after all this, must be a terrible experience."

Then I noticed Ricky Williams. He was half smiling, half smirking. "Yeah," he said softly. "A horrible experience."

I wished I'd stayed quiet.

The St. Louis Cardinals have the distinction of being the oldest, continuously run professional football franchise in the nation. And, from their beginning in 1898, when the team was a little football group on the south side of Chicago, they have been notably tightfisted.

Long before I was drafted by the Cardinals, money has been a team issue, from the front office to the coaches to the players. Not to say that's all bad. When you're running a business, the bottom line speaks the loudest, and clearly, professional football is big business. But I went from fun football at Portland State to business brutality in the NFL overnight, and I wasn't skilled at playing hardball with the management yet. I was still sporting my "win one for the Gipper" college attitude; to heck with money, I wanted to play.

Leigh tried to bridle my enthusiasm for obvious reasons, but much of his early advice fell on deaf ears. He was asking for a $120,000 signing bonus and a $90,000 salary. The Cardinals were offering a $90,000 bonus and a $64,000 salary, and Leigh wasn't budging. "Neil," he said, "they know they got a first-round pick in you for nothing. But you can't back down."

But Leigh, unlike most agents, didn't believe in keeping his players out of mini-camp just because they hadn't come to terms. In fact, he's against holdouts altogether if they can be prevented. But he was fearing the worst with the Cardinals; just two years earlier, while representing running back Theotis Brown, another second-round pick, Leigh had engaged in one of his bloodiest contract wars ever with the St. Louis organization. "I'm not looking forward to this," he assured me.

But despite their reputation, I wanted very much to play for the Cardinals after being picked. This was an historic team, a team that had touched all ages of time. In 1920, it was one of the eleven charter members of the American Professional Football League. The Cardinals won their first NFL title in 1925 when the established league expanded to twenty teams.

After being purchased by Chicago dentist Dr. David Jones in 1929, the team was finally acquired by Charles W. Bidwill, father of the present owner, William V. Bidwill. It went on to witness the "dream" backfield of the forties, which consisted of Paul Christman, Marshall Goldberg, Pat Harder, and Charley Trippi. The quartet led the Cards to a 28-21 NFL championship over the Philadelphia Eagles in 1947. The elder Bidwill died in April 1947, and ownership was passed to sons Charles Jr. and William, who moved the team to St. Louis in 1960. But William V. Bidwill became the sole owner in 1972, and on July 1, 1979, incorporation of the company was accomplished.

Mr. Bidwill, a Chicago native, is a shrewd businessman; his success at everything but football proves it. A short, heavy-set man with slicked-back hair, Mr. Bidwill has puppy eyes, hidden behind tinted bifocals. In 1978, Mr. Bidwill hired Bud Wilkinson as his head coach. Wilkinson, who did win 139 college games at Oklahoma, had never coached in the pros, and for that matter, hadn't coached for ten years when Bidwill hired him. All-Pro offensive lineman Dan Dierdorf, who rode out several stormy St. Louis coaching moves, was very outspoken at the time. "The team was disintegrating," he told *Sport* magazine. "Our basic problem is players [are] openly critical of management . . . you can't discuss something with Bidwill. He's shy. He'll walk past a player and look down rather than say hello." Dan's description couldn't have been more fitting. Others, however, weren't so polite. "Bill Bidwill is petty and unbelievably cheap," says a former St. Louis coach. "And director of operations Joe Sullivan is his buffer, and he has the same wonderful qualities as Bidwill." Bud Wilkinson admitted he was shocked at the way the Cardinals operated during his first year, but stuck around for another year "because of the excitement of coaching in the NFL." However, Mr. Bidwill fired him with two games left in the 1979 season. This prompted another uproar in the media. In August of 1980 *Sport* reported:

> Bidwill's firings and general meddling so far have not brought success. [The Cardinals] are a team that might do well if it ever settled down to the simple pleasures of playing football.

The Cardinals did win division titles in 1974 and 1975, but lost early both times in the play-offs. After Wilkinson, Mr. Bidwill's next choice was Jim Hanifan, whom he hired on January 30, 1980. Hanifan, a popular offensive assistant with the Big Red for the previous four years, took over the head coaching duties with high regard from the players. He had the unenviable task of trying to dispel all the unrest that surrounded the club, but he was fighting history. When I first arrived, along with E. J. Junior shortly after the draft, he was among the first to greet me. Coach Hanifan had finished 5-11 in his first year, but the team's development gave reason for optimism, particularly with the strength of the new drafts. Hanifan originally joined the Cardinals in 1973 as offensive line coach under Don Coryell, and remained in that capacity through 1978. His 1975 offensive line set an NFL record by allowing the fewest quarterback sacks (8) in a season. In 1977, he was named NFL assistant coach of the year.

Coach Hanifan worked at the high-school, junior-college, and major-college levels before turning to the pros. His last college term began in 1972, when he joined Coryell at San Diego State and worked with the offensive line for two years before coming to the Cardinals in 1973. So management considered him well-schooled in the passing game and a leader, as well. A perfect gentleman, he was never overbearing, but in my opinion, he lacked firmness. Unlike Mouse, he never seemed to absolutely be in charge of the program. But who was I, a brash young rookie, to be forming opinions about the head coach? I made up my mind to simply do as I was told.

Mini-camp is a three- or four-day ritual held once or twice during the spring by nearly every pro team, during which time rookies are acquainted with the pro system and veterans are given refresher courses. This is not to be confused with training camp, which is the full-fledged, month-long ordeal in July and August which immediately precedes the start of the season.

The first part of mini-camp is generally for rookies and free agents only, and they are joined by the veterans later in the week. For the veteran, mini-camp is just another annoying problem in the off-season. For the rookie, however, it is the first in a series of auditions to impress the coaches and retool your thinking about football. Players wear only helmets, T-shirts, and shorts, but coaches can tell a lot about athletic ability long before the pads are ever donned.

Coaches view mini-camp as an opportunity to tell players how to prepare for training camp, to begin putting in the offense and defense, and to reacquaint the veterans and indoctrinate the rookies and free agents on how the team organizes its practices and meetings. Although the coaches begin brainwashing you with new theories and principles from the beginning, the fundamentals of football remain the same; thus, anyone with a football background is basically familiar with the drills they're put through. First comes the 40-yard dash, the yardstick in the NFL. Then agility drills, such as running around traffic cones and back-pedaling routines. Linemen are asked to fire off a three-point stance into heavy tackling dummies, then bounce off, spin, and hit another bag. Coaches film the camps from start to finish and use the captured images—bad or good—as training camp nears to help decide which guys will get early plane tickets home. The official decision, however, is usually never made until camp.

From the first day, things were obviously much different than Portland State. My days of taking a two- or three-step rollout when passing were over. "Drop straight back," Harry Gilmer, our offensive coordinator, said, viewing me skeptically with arms crossed and one finger pressed to his lips. Harry was a weathered old pro who'd been around the NFL a quarter of a century and tutoring St. Louis quarterbacks since 1967. The coaches asked for a seven-yard drop, which is quite an unnatural act. Imagine running backwards as fast as you can, then trying to stop and throw the ball forward. Quarterbacks have done it for years, but Mouse's system sure was easier after having used it for four years. The pro way is known as the "drop and set," in which you move straight back while looking downfield, set up, then step forward while throwing the ball.

The most important thing in the dropback is the first step; it is crucial to a successful play. Often your own offensive linemen, who are backing up in pass protection, can step on your feet if you don't get out from under center fast enough. You have to get away in a hurry. The coaches watched me carefully as I practiced backing away from the line.

"Don't take a false step," Harry Gilmer ordered. Most quarterbacks, including myself, usually take a short false step forward with their right foot before dropping back to pass. The reason, I guess, is to gain some extra drive. Although your drop looks better without it, most quarterbacks, including Joe Namath and Terry Bradshaw have taken the false jab step throughout their careers. Next time you're watching football, watch the quarterback right before he drops to throw; at the snap, his left foot will more than likely step quickly forward before he backs away. Most still do it today. While coaches urge youngsters not to do it, unless a quarterback is horribly slow of foot it usually doesn't hurt anything.

Once you get going back at full speed, you have to come to a full stop on your back leg, which almost bounces you back in the other direction to give you the momentum to throw the ball. Coaches call this a gather step—you plant the back foot, gather it under you to get your balance, and then move in the direction of your target. Which means a right-handed quarterback will take two steps to throw the ball; one when they gather their right leg under them and another when they step forward with their left leg to throw.

Although the rookie camp lasted just three days, I felt I was catching on rather quickly. The coaches were outwardly pleased with my progress. The most notable difference in the pros was the lack of personal rapport. Few coaches get involved in, or care about, your personal life. It is a business, a job, and they are only concerned with your performance on the field. But I was taking smooth drops by the end of the three-day session, and the smiles on their faces, coupled with their telltale winks to one another, were all the assurance I needed. I felt I was making quick progress toward the number-two job, ahead of veteran backups Rusty Lisch and Mike Lloyd.

In a rare moment, Coach Hanifan ambled over to me, his red St. Louis windbreaker flapping in the breeze.

"You're picking up things pretty quick," he said.

"Thanks," I replied, not exactly sure what to say.

"You sure are way ahead of most rookies at reading defensive coverages," he added.

"You can thank Mouse Davis for that," I said. Hanifan smirked.

Confidence was coming slowly, but it was coming. When mini-camp ended, I knew I could play on this level, and I was hungry for July to arrive.

Because of my strong mini-camp showing, my feeling was the Cardinals would probably loosen up the pursestrings a little. Wrong. Negotiations between Leigh and the front office were not just slow, they were dead, a fact which obviously left me distressed. Worse, several team situations made great ammunition for the media, and they didn't hesitate to use it. You can imagine my feelings when I picked up the NFL preview copy of *Inside Sports*, hoping to read something positive and found this instead:

> ... Cards continued drafting well by netting linebacker E. J. Junior for the weak linebacker corps and Neil Lomax to inherit Jim Hart's QB job. When (defensive back) Carl Allen was injured last season, the secondary became all-white, an NFL rarity. After the Giants' Phil Simms torched them for five TDs last year, a St. Louis black newspaper scolded them in a head-

line: "It Takes Brothers To Catch Brothers." Bitterness lingers
from salary disputes. As fast as he is, (running back) O. J. Anderson can't outrun all that.

In one preview alone, writer Gary Smith had touched on some
sensitive, and at the same time, ill-founded, points. The salary
disputes were certainly an ongoing problem, but I wasn't ready
for a quarterback controversy with Jim Hart, the Cardinals' aging
leader. And I sure didn't want the team being disrupted over any
racial issues; charges had been made the year before that coaches
were prejudiced. I was stepping into a lion's den, a situation I
wasn't particularly happy about.

Leigh, however, was already doing battle in a long series of
telephone calls from his Berkeley office to St. Louis. He was dealing with Joe Sullivan, a front-office man in his fifties who prided
himself on long, hard negotiations. Joe looks exactly the way he
talks and acts. He starts out surly and burly and goes downhill
from there, like he always has a chip on his shoulder. I was glad it
was Leigh and not me who had to talk to the guy.

Little by little, I was beginning to understand what Leigh had
told me, even prior to the draft. Sullivan often refused to return
Leigh's phone calls and was very one-sided about the negotiations. In early conversations with Leigh he had berated his morals
and legal technique, calling him "a bloodsucker . . . you're an af-
fliction on the human race." Then he hung up.

When fans read about holdouts and negotiations in the papers
they don't understand all the details. We hear things like, "How
could he do that to the *team?*" The fans don't see how the players are teated. We're nothing but spokes in the wheel of a giant
moneymaking machine, and the owners and management always
appear to be the good guys. "They know a young guy wants to
play," Leigh said. "That's why they do this. They let you sit and
sit and sit, wondering if they'll ever call. A team seldom makes a
decent offer until the last minute. They work on your psyche;
they know football players just want to play football. But you
have to be mentally tough. You have to think about your future
or you'll be playing for nothing."

Leigh kept trying. One morning, after being up working the

entire night before, Leigh got a rare phone call from Sullivan. Leigh was dead tired, but Joe was in rare form. He really seemed to enjoy his role as the rock thrower for the front office. Once again, Joe made his subpar offer. Once again, Leigh, exhausted, flatly refused.

"You should be disbarred for doing this kind of work," Sullivan screamed into the phone. "You leech . . . you vulture . . . you're crazy . . . you're worthless. Neil wants to play for this team, and you're the only thing keeping him from it."

"Yeah," Leigh argued, "but long after the excitement of playing for an NFL team fades, the sorry numbers on his contract won't be fading. He'll be the starting quarterback, and you know it. It's a matter of time."

"He's nothing but a second-round pick," Sullivan retorted, seething into the phone. "You take your offer and stick it where the sun doesn't shine. Lomax is so overrated it isn't funny. So there. You can either take this money, or Neil can sit in your office until hell freezes over."

Bam. End of conversation. It was going to be a long summer. And I thought football was just a game?

Back home in Portland, all my relatives were celebrating my recent success. My parents had already started a collection of St. Louis Cardinals attire, and the phone lines to the Lomax household stayed hot as my career was discussed with every friend and relative this side of the Mississippi. I was still mostly just awed by what was happening, and I was overcome by how fast it all was taking place.

All my life I'd wanted a BMW. To me, it was the finest car made, and I loved its looks. Leigh had advised me to buy a toy and get it out of my system. "People can better contain the crazy feeling of spending once they have a decent car, a decent stereo, and a decent house," he said. The stereo and house would have to wait until I signed a contract, but the car I could go ahead and buy. Using my earnings from the Senior Bowl as a down payment, I financed a beautiful gray 320 BMW, complete with St.

Louis Cardinals license plate frame on the back. I was sure my soon-to-be-arriving pro paychecks would more than cover the monthly payment.

Stuart loved the car. The day I got it we rode around the Portland State campus again and again, stereo playing, windows rolled down. I felt on top of the world. At the time, Stuart was trying to accept my good fortune, but he was struggling. "You sure are lucky, Neil," he said, touching the dash of the $17,000 car and fiddling with stereo knobs. "The pros. Maybe one day I'll join you."

With his team depleted of seniors and virtually no goals left to conquer at Portland State, Mouse had decided to take the offensive coordinator's position at U. of C. Stuart had been redshirted immediately after his knee injury, meaning he would play for PSU one more year . . . in the absence of all his friends. The new coach, Don Read, was a run-oriented guy, and his offense could not match the excitement of the Run 'n' Shoot. Stu knew he was in for a long year, which made me feel worse. I was happy for the things happening in my life, but it was a sick feeling to see Stu in such unrest.

Leo Marty, our trainer, was afraid Stu's knee wasn't sufficiently healed. But Stu had never been one for the weight room. Meanwhile, several other guys from the team—some with less ability than Stu—had been given tryouts with professional teams. Joel Sigel, the fullback, had gone to the Raiders, and Clint Didier, a 6-6 wide receiver, to the Redskins. Stu, however, who had been the best receiver in the nation just eighteen months earlier, found himself on a team with a young quarterback and a running offense; he felt like a milk bucket under a bull. All the circumstances were forcing changes in Stu, and I just couldn't figure out the words to say to him. "You know I should be right there with you," he'd say, staring off into space. "I helped you get where you are. A lot of your passes would've been dropped without me." He would laugh, but I knew he was serious deep down.

Stu's bitterness had given him a horrible temperament. That summer the *Oregon Journal* featured him, and he provided great copy. He talked about his problems, how his old teammates had virtually abandoned him, and how little he had left. His life had become a puzzle, and several pieces were clearly missing. The story appeared under the headline "Gaussoin Can't Put It All in One Basket Anymore," and quoted him at length about the last four years. Nothing outwardly negative was said, but his confusion was obvious. Inside, Stu was crying out for help, but I, for one, didn't really know how to help him. "Sometimes I can't sleep at night, asking myself, *What is the right plan for me?*" he told the paper. It was an awkward situation for me. I almost wanted to apologize to Stu for my success.

Nevertheless, with my first training camp only months away, I was riding high. The big time had finally arrived, and I hadn't even signed a contract yet. Everything was fine until Mitch found out about my car purchase from my sister, Val. He called me and was quite open about his disappointment.

"You what?" he demanded. "That's the stupidest thing I've ever heard of. Mom and Dad can't even afford decent clothes, and you're driving around in a $17,000 car. Mom and Dad have needed a car for years now, and all they can talk about is how you immediately thought of yourself. Great, Neil, just great. You're losing it, you know that? You're losing control of this situation."

"I earned it," I argued. "I wasn't showing off. I've always liked BMWs, and you know it. It's just a car, for heaven's sake. Get off my back."

I could feel he was fuming on the other end of the line.

"You better learn to be thankful, Neil," he said. "First Timothy 6:6, 7, clearly says that 'godliness with contentment is great gain . . . for we brought nothing into this world, and it is certain we can carry nothing out.' And later in that same chapter, we're told that 'they that will be rich fall into temptation and a snare, and into many foolish and hurtful lusts, which drown men in destruction and perdition' (v. 9). Get a grip on yourself. There's nowhere for you to go from here except downward unless you get this thing under control."

Wow. Although Mitch had gone a little overboard, he made

his point. For the record, I still own that same BMW today—it's now six years old. Even though I felt justified in buying a new car, buying such an expensive one before I'd even adjusted to the NFL made it clear my reasoning was wrong. I could see, through Mitch, that just that one instance of flaunting had wounded my friends and family. Without trying, I made others feel like I was towering over them, like I was showboating my success. After Mitch's strong suggestions, I understood how the abuse of cash—whether purposely or accidentally—could quickly ruin relationships.

Football had truly become a business. My parents were very interested in when I would sign, how much I would get, and how I felt about my new income. "I don't have a new income yet," I kept reminding them. I sensed the role I was being shoved into, and I didn't like it. Everything that had seemed so good was blowing up in my face. With confusion swirling about me— the negotiations with the Cardinals, the financial and spiritual turmoil of my family, and just the pressure of my upcoming first season—I sought out Ron Kincaid and some spiritual counseling.

Ron was preparing to become pastor of Sunset Presbyterian Church. Before he left Mountain Park, however, he invited me to participate in a summer mission program where the church would minister to a local community for a week, then move on to another one. I joined him in Hermiston, Oregon, where we did Vacation Bible School projects. It was a very emotional time, as I had been close friends with Ron for the last six years, and I felt as though an era was coming to an end. But it was a good opportunity for me to air my feelings and frustration, and a lot of our free time was spent discussing how I would cope with my pro career. I had lots of questions, and I pressed Ron for answers.

"Neil, your commitment to Christ long preceded your fame," he said. "You have a spiritual maturity, even if you're unsure about everything else. If a person is not mature—in other words, if he doesn't know his faith and is not strong with the Lord—he will become enamored with the fame and riches. I think you're holding up pretty well, with an exception or two. But we all make a few mistakes. You're human, like the rest of us."

"But how do I deal with my family?" I asked. "I'm not trying to alienate anybody. I just feel like I'm being substituted for God. Instead of looking to God, it's going to be easy for others to look to me for answers, because I'm going to have a few extra dollars in my pocket. I don't want people befriending me or getting close to me in hopes of a monetary gift here and there. I know it's better to give than receive, but not when people treat you like Yosemite Sam, fresh from a gold rush."

Ron smiled warmly and opened his Bible. His soft tone was comforting, as always, but his biblical wisdom hit harder than a blitzing linebacker.

" 'Trust in the Lord with all thine heart; and lean not unto thine own understanding,' " he read gently. " 'In all thy ways acknowledge him, and he shall direct thy paths' (Proverbs 3:5, 6).

"Neil, seek God's will," Ron continued. "Just like you have since high school. Base every decision you make on the principles found in the Word of God. These are life-changing decisions. Only you can make them. Don't dare make them alone.

"Trust in God, Neil. Trust in God."

It was a very tough, transitional summer. Ron, a cornerstone in my relationship with Christ, was leaving for another church. Mouse, who had been like a father to me the last four years, had moved to another state. In weeks, I would move to St. Louis for my first professional season. Almost everybody I knew was claiming some responsibility for my success. Relatives and friends were expecting financial gifts when I signed. Too often people perceive money to be the answer to all problems. My refusal to make promises of financial gifts before I even signed a contract, brought accusations of cheapness, stinginess, and lack of concern. That couldn't have been further from the truth, but I could see that family relationships were already being threatened. My heart was crying out to be treated like "just Neil." Meanwhile, St.

Louis papers were touting me as the answer to the Cardinals' age-old problems. A quarterback controversy was brewing, and camp hadn't even started. The best of my career was ahead of me, yet I never felt more confused. It was a lot for me to handle, physically, emotionally, and spiritually. Despite my frequent talks with the Lord, I felt completely alone. My biggest opportunity was threatening to engulf me.

It was July 14, 1981, and training camp was set to start the next day. Leigh was at his Los Angeles home, sitting by the side of his pool under the morning sunshine, tossing a ball to his dog. Leigh is the most relaxed lawyer that's ever been. He seldom gets ruffled over any situation, but if he does, there's trouble. Attired in swimming trunks and a T-shirt, he walked through the sliding glass door into his den and returned with a yellow legal pad and a telephone with a cord long enough to stretch around the entire swimming pool.

He dialed the phone.

"May I speak to Joe Sullivan, please?" he asked nicely.

Seconds later the phone rattled and the St. Louis Cardinals' personnel man picked up the call. "Yeah," Sullivan answered rudely. One thing you can say for Sullivan: He's consistent. Every day, 365 days out of the year, the man gets up on the wrong side of the bed. Which is why, I guess, he's such a good negotiator.

"Your so-called final offer is not acceptable," Leigh said politely. "Training camp starts tomorrow, and my guy won't be there unless we can come to terms real soon."

Leigh may as well have slapped Sullivan in the face.

"You're lying to Neil, you little runt," he said, his voice gradually getting louder. "You couldn't get a decent job anywhere else, so you became an agent. What do you think you are, anyway? Do you actually think I respect your demands?"

"I'm not asking for your respect, sir," Leigh said, obviously irritated but still under control. "I'm merely asking you for a decent offer."

Leigh was on his feet now, pacing around the pool.

"Why do you have to be like this, you worm?" Sullivan roared still getting louder. "You're not getting anything from me."

"Why does every conversation with you end up a name-calling session?" Leigh demanded, angrier now. His pace around the pool was picking up speed. "Why can't you get along with any agent? Why do you think you have these problems with every lawyer you deal with? Reasonable men can have reasonable differences and still have a reasonable working relationship!"

"Oh, yeah?" rumbled Sullivan, his voice reaching a violent crescendo. "Well who says I have to be reasonable? What makes you think I even care about you or your stupid quarterback? We don't need Neil Lomax! We don't need Leigh Steinberg! Jim Hart's been here seventeen years and he's as healthy as a rookie!"

"Why did you pick Neil, then?" retorted Leigh. "You drafted him. You wanted him. He's not the one who decided to play in St. Louis, and I certainly didn't put him in St. Louis. You, Mr. Sullivan, your franchise wanted Neil. We had nothing to do with the decision. The coaches are all impressed with him. He's done great in mini-camps. And you don't even want to give him a decent bonus, a bonus that's in line with the other draft picks of his ability."

"If Neil Lomax is so great, then why did so many teams *not* pick him, you twerp?" Sullivan bellowed. "I ought to wring your neck."

"Are you threatening me?" Leigh asked.

"That does it," fired back Sullivan. "We've made our last offer. I'm through trying to negotiate."

"*Negotiate?*" Leigh said, his voice rising to a high whine. "You haven't negotiated, you've merely harassed me. Maybe the Canadian Football League will be interested in Neil. They won't treat us like this in Canada."

Leigh knew I had absolutely no interest in playing in Canada; he was merely baiting Sullivan. To no avail, I might add.

"You take your guy to Canada," screamed Sullivan. "We don't need him."

"It's just a matter of time before Neil is the starting quarter-back and you know it," Leigh reiterated. Leigh was furious. A man can only take so much harassment before he reaches the breaking point, and Leigh was clearly there.

"We *have* a starting quarterback," Sullivan spit. "I've had it. We're offering $64,000, a $90,000 bonus, and that's final. I don't care if the kid never plays another down of football in his life."

Bam. Another "bargaining session" had come to an end.

I was concerned. Like any youngster, all I wanted to do was play. I told Leigh that the money was getting less and less impor-tant.

"Now it is," Leigh said, "because you want to play. But a year from now, when you're the starting quarterback and you're bound to a horrible contract, you're gonna regret jumping ahead."

I was like a kid before Christmas. Back home in Portland, I couldn't sit still. I'd watch a few minutes of television, then jump up and do something else. I was always working out, lifting weights or throwing the ball. I wanted to play. The day camp opened, I wasn't there. I couldn't stand the pressure. What I didn't realize is that this is nothing but a psychological ploy used by the team. Few football players can stand to be sitting at home when their teammates are playing—a fact every general manager is well aware of.

I packed my bags, hoping a decision would be made. Nothing. I couldn't stand the silence. It was driving me crazy. Besides, I didn't want to make anybody mad; I was hoping to make a good impression as a rookie. Finally, I broke down and called Leigh.

"Maybe we'd get somewhere if I called Sullivan myself," I said. Leigh chuckled. "Neil, that's out of your department," he answered.

"I want to play."

"If you want to talk to Joe, go ahead. But be prepared. You're not dealing with a den mother for the girl scouts. Just be polite, state your demands, and let him know you're not afraid."

I called him.

After introducing myself, I stuck to my guns. In rapid-fire fashion, I made it clear that I wanted to play for the Cardinals. I told
him my brief holdout could've been prevented with some
old-fashioned give-and-take.

"This is ridiculous," I said. "What's the big deal?"

Sullivan sneered at my innocence. To him, I was like fresh
meat thrown into the tiger cage at the city zoo.

"Your attorney says he needs more money, and we aren't giving you another dime," he groused.

I could sense my face reddening. These guys play for keeps.
Assertively, I gave him both barrels.

"Look, pal, you guys can afford it, so why don't you give us
what we want and we'll be done with it?"

With the precision of a heart surgeon, Sullivan carved me into
little pieces.

"It's not the principle of affording things," he explained curtly.
"Just because you can afford to go out and buy a Mercedes, if you
don't need it, it's not practical. Right?"

I found myself nodding in agreement and thinking uneasily
about my new BMW.

"Well, Neil, we don't want to pay more than what's practical
for a second-round pick."

Period. Thus ended my brief tenure as my own agent.

I called Leigh and told him I'd gotten absolutely nowhere, but
that I was going to sign anyway. "I can't take the suspense. I want
to play and that's it." Leigh made another phone call to the Cardinals (against his will) and succeeded at working a deal that
would allow us to renegotiate at the end of the season if I was the
starting quarterback by year's end. That was the only allowance
they would give us.

"Well, you're on your way," Leigh said. "A ticket to St. Louis
is waiting for you at the airport. Good luck. And don't hold any
of this negotiating business against your coaches. You take a positive attitude, be polite to everybody, and remember, the coaches
had nothing to do with this. If you need me, call. It's up to you
now."

The four-hour flight to St. Louis was tiring. I had dressed casually and looked slightly ridiculous in my open-collar golf shirt, Levis, and thongs. But I had worked hard in preparation for this moment, and I was ready. When I stepped from the plane, I was mobbed by reporters.

"Quarterback hopeful Neil Lomax is arriving in St. Louis to sign with the team and report to training camp," shouted one television reporter as a live camera followed my every move. Cameras flashed. I blinked, watching blue spots fade before my eyes. Microphones were thrust in my face. "I'm ready to play," I said, catching my balance after being jostled by newspeople as I waded through the terminal. "Let's go do it. I'm here, and I'm ready to play some football."

A team assistant met me in the lobby and we finally escaped from the airport. It seemed like no time before I was seated in the Cardinals' offices, where my big moment arrived. A stack of papers, bound at the top was handed to me, along with a pen. The words *Standard Player Contract* were emblazoned across the top in bold letters.

With great relief, I signed the dotted line. *From this point on,* I thought, *I do my talking on the field.*

Even at nine I was dreaming of
playing professional football.

My tenth birthday
brought a new bicycle.

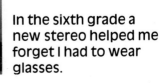

In the sixth grade a
new stereo helped me
forget I had to wear
glasses.

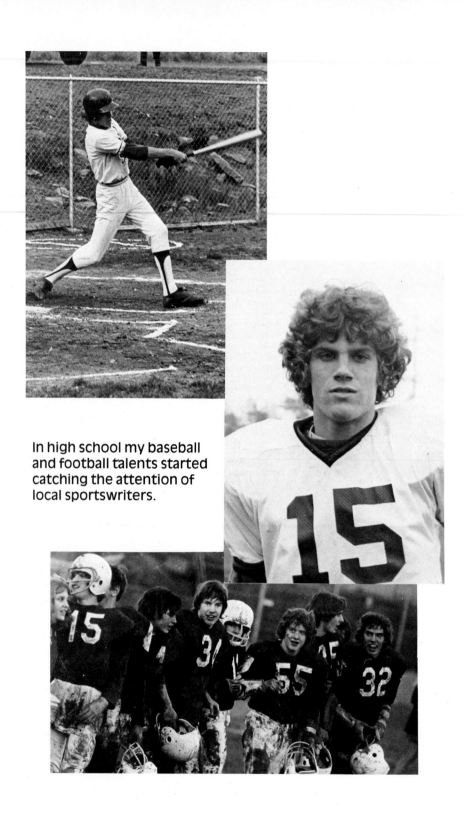

In high school my baseball and football talents started catching the attention of local sportswriters.

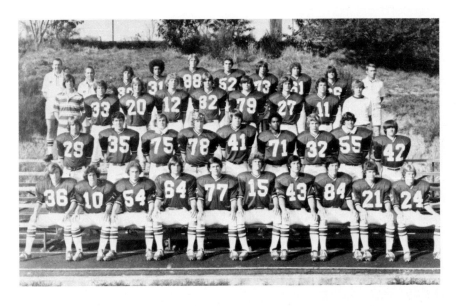

By my senior year
I was on the varsity football and baseball teams.

PSU teammate Dave Semantel and I after a record-breaking game against Idaho State.

My brother Terry was the "Mouse" at PSU

The other Mouse in my life: Coach Darrell Davis.

My first professional game—the East-West Shrine Game.

On the sidelines or right in the center, playing for the Cardinals has never been dull.

(Bottom) *Left to right:* Lee Nelson, Pat Tilley, Ken Greene, and I after beating the Chargers in November 1983.

Former PSU quarterbacks: June Jones, Terry Summerfield, and I.

The newlyweds in
Hawaii for Pro Bowl '85.

Laurie and I on our wedding
day, February 9, 1985.

The Lomax men at my wed-
ding: Mitch, Dad, the happy
groom, and Terry.

Off the field, I just relax.

(Bottom) Our first "baby," Samson, at ten weeks old.

8

Daniel in the Lion's Den

"It's amazing what the human body can do when chased by a bigger human body."

—Jack Thompson, former NFL quarterback

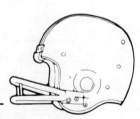

"Hey, rookie," a voice yelled. "Sing, boy." I looked over my shoulder. The deep voice belonged to Dan Dierdorf, a veteran offensive lineman who weighed over 280 pounds. I swallowed hard. Making rookies sing for their dinners is a training camp ritual, and veterans derive a lot of pleasure from making scared young men sing before an audience of bellowing, crude, huge men. Most rookies, voices shaking, stand up as they're told,

129

sometimes on the table, and blurt out a few lines. Others are bold, adding dancing routines or skits to their acts. Still others drop their heads closer to their food, ignoring the demands of the veterans. That, I might add, is not a wise move. Many a rookie has found himself bruised and beaten, or, worse, the victim of endless practical jokes, because he didn't obey when first asked to sing.

"Lomax!" Dierdorf roared, "I said sing, *boy.*"

I pushed away from the table and stood up. Smiling, I cleared my throat, then ducked a piece of bread that flew in my direction. It's easy to be intimidated, but I gave my menacing-looking teammates a cocky grin.

"Jesus loves me this I know," I began, trying not to laugh. "For the Bible tells me soooooo . . ."

My voice was drowned out by the boos and catcalls from the crowd. By now, the air was filled with flying objects. I was weaving and bobbing like a boxer, trying not to get hit by a tomato here, a piece of fruit there.

"Little ones to Him belong . . ."

"Sit down, Lomax!" yelled defensive lineman Stafford Mays. "You better be glad you're a quarterback, 'cause you sure as hell aren't a singer!"

I sat down. Dave Stief, my former PSU teammate and a three-year Cardinals veteran, was laughing next to me. "You were great," Dave said. "Just great. But you better learn some other songs. They'll be leaving you alone."

In the few days I'd been at training camp, Dave had been a great asset. He filled me in on the do's and don't of camp and really took me under his wing. Before the first dinner, he had warned me to be prepared to sing. "Don't make a big deal out of it," he said. "Just do what they tell you to do, and you'll be fine." After the last afternoon practice, some rookies would shower and rush to the dinner hall, hurriedly eat, and leave, just to avoid being singled out. Others would wait until the last ten or fifteen minutes before the cafeteria closed, giving the veterans time to leave. It was really an uncomfortable situation. I went with Dave, but I admit my dinner was ruined a few times because my stomach was in knots. The food, though, was the best thing about camp. There was enough food to feed an army. I'd never seen more good food in my life—thick brown steaks, fresh fish, sizzling lobster, juicy fresh fruit. It was like dying and waking up in a culinary heaven.

Training camp was held at Lindenwood College in St. Charles, Missouri (just outside of St. Louis), in furnacelike heat. The humidity was incredible; my shirt would get soaked in sweat from just standing outside. Thundershowers were a daily occurrence and merely added to the miserable conditions. You'd think for a pro football team, we'd have better practice facilities. Only one field, with astroturf, is available, and it is situated down in a hole at the west end of the school. The temperature on the field hovered between 110 and 120 degrees every day. A guy could melt away in conditions like these.

My first two nights at camp I didn't get any sleep; my air conditioner was broken and I was too shy to complain or say anything until the third day. Believe me, I was glad to be there, humidity and all. The second night, in fact, I snuck down to Dave's room and slept on the floor next to him. The next day, backup quarterback Mike Lloyd got cut, and I asked for his room and they obliged. Having air conditioning never felt better.

My first two purchases in the pros were a clock radio and a big padlock, which I used to bolt my door. I had been told that veterans were known to come by rookies' rooms and do "unmentionable" things to them, like beating them up or shaving their heads. I didn't want that to happen to me; over the years, I've developed a great fondness for the well-being of my body. "We have a few jerks on the team who might try something like that," Dave admitted. "The padlock might be overdoing it a little, but it isn't a bad idea."

I was making real progress in practice, and my training under Mouse was paying off. The whole experience was a rush—pro football, lots of money, groupies, and an exciting life-style. It's obvious how easy it is for a guy to be consumed by it all, but I was fighting to remember my daily devotions and the lessons Ron Kincaid had pounded into my head over the years.

Our first exhibition game was in San Diego. It was exhilarating just be be standing on the sidelines of a professional team. I was standing there wearing a baseball hat, carrying a clipboard and charting plays, and yelling encouragement to my teammates. I got in late in the game with the other rookies, and though I didn't do anything too impressive, I enjoyed just being there. I completed a couple of passes to Dave and moved the team for its only points in the fourth quarter. I felt pretty good about it, but my bubble burst only hours after the San Diego game, when I had my first real run-in with the management.

Our next game was in Seattle, and the coaches had decided to give us two days off after San Diego, which was a Saturday game, and resume training camp in Seattle for a week before the Seahawks game. The team was supposed to fly out to Seattle and settle in at the training site immediately following the San Diego game. Kenny Greene, one of my teammates and also a Portland area resident, had a pilot friend who owned his own Cessna. Kenny arranged to have Dave and me fly home with him so we could spend the weekend with our families. The pilot planned to meet us in Seattle when our team plane arrived at the airport. On August 3, the federal air traffic controllers had gone on national strike after their union had rejected the government's final offer for a new contract, and Seattle's main international airport was closed. So we were told we would have to fly into Boeing Field, a smaller airport north of the city. We relayed the information to Kenny's friend and he agreed to meet us there around 1:00 A.M.

I was excited about going home for a few days, for several reasons. Besides looking forward to seeing my family, Leigh had helped me purchase a house—for living and tax purposes—since I'd been in camp, and I had some friends from church living there for the season.

The whole time I'd been in camp, I'd heard horror stories about dealing with the management, and even though I felt I'd been dealt a crooked deck with my contract, I still didn't think the guys in the front office were that bad. "Wait 'till you've been around a while," Dave kept saying. His words were a prophecy. You can imagine our surprise when the team's charter landed at Seattle International Airport, not Boeing Field, as we had been told. Kenny's friend and his plane were at Boeing Field, and because of the strike, we were told there was no way to reach him and explain the situation. When we came down off the charter flight into the terminal, Joe Sullivan was standing there, wearing his patented smug grin.

Kenny walked right up to him. "Why didn't you tell me we weren't flying into Boeing Field?" he demanded. Sullivan casually lit a cigarette and blew smoke in Kenny's direction. "We told everybody who is somebody," he said curtly. Kenny lunged for the director of personnel, and Dave and I held him back. Getting close to Sullivan's face, Kenny screamed in anger. "My friends are waiting at the other airport, and you know it," he said, as I fought to keep him away from Sullivan. Sullivan laughed at him, which made Kenny madder. "I hate you, man," he roared. Chuckling, Sullivan turned and walked away.

Reaching Kenny's friend proved impossible. We finally ended up getting a commercial flight to Portland around 4:00 A.M. Until then, I'd had no real direct contact with Sullivan except one phone call, but suddenly I realized why Leigh disliked him. That solidified everything Leigh had said. "He's a jerk," Dave said. I agreed. How people like Sullivan get into positions of management, with the power to affect people's lives and jobs, I'll never know. "It's a business," Dave said later. "The management doesn't care about you, or how you feel, or what kind of a person you are. The only thing management cares about is whether you put points on the board."

If the Seattle trip was any indication, Dave was right. Mouse Davis and my warm, friendly days at Portland State seemed so far away. I missed that feeling.

Watching Jim Hart, the Cardinals' incumbent quarterback, was like watching history in the making. Barely over six feet tall, handsome and articulate, at thirty-seven years of age the sixteen-

year veteran looked more like a lawyer than a quarterback. The
slight gray around his temples gave away his age, despite his baby
face. Hart's career had been helped by his being in the right place
at the right time; and he made the most out of every chance. In
1966, he had earned a reserve spot on the team after signing as an
undrafted free agent out of Southern Illinois, and sporting annals
at the time called him "a long shot . . . certainly not the man of
the future for the Cards." But in 1967, four days before the season opener, starting quarterback Charley Johnson was called into
the Army, and Jim was named the starter, a job he would hold for
nearly the next two decades.

Jimmy really didn't have that much of an arm by the time I
came to St. Louis. He could still put the ball on the money with
the underneath stuff, but ask him to go deep, and it required
most all the strength he could muster. The arm that had carried
him to four Pro Bowls and countless team and NFL career
records was giving way to the relentless passing of time. Jim had
survived young rookies before, and none had taken his job. But
from day one, he had little to say to me, if anything, and when I
started whipping routine 30- or 40-yard bullets, I caught Jim
watching occasionally. He had never had the arm strength I possessed. I sensed he feared for his job.

He was a much different guy than I had thought he would be.
Jim had been around a long time, but he didn't parade around
like an egotist or a big-time quarterback. My first impression was
that he had a lot of bitterness. He seldom had much to say,
whether it was the coaches, the management, or the other players.
It was like he came to camp carrying a grudge. So not only was he
another year older, but he also was being challenged for his job.

If anyone had taken my talents for granted because I was from
"tiny" Portland State, they soon realized they were badly mistaken. I'd gained more knowledge of reading defenses and knowing how to attack a defense under Mouse Davis than most of the
quarterbacks at the big schools had. I'm not sure exactly what was
going through Jim's mind, except that when he would watch me
take snaps in practice he knew I was a player. And I was ready to
give Jim a run for his money. When I asked him questions, he an-

swered with short, curt answers; never smart-alecky or sarcastically, just brief and soft, as if he really didn't have much to say. The tension built all through training camp, although the local media and coaches were saying I was probably four or five years away from being a good NFL quarterback. My brash, forward style of handling situations obviously didn't help matters, and Jim wasn't fond of my "cockiness." People who meet me for the first time sometimes think I'm overly aggressive, too confident. About the most he ever openly said about me was that I was "a little big in my boots to be just out of Portland State."

The rest of the preseason went pretty quickly. Mitch got married the night of our final exhibition game against the Bears, which we lost 31-27. I phoned him and his new bride, the former Allison Rogers, in Portland after the game and issued my congratulations. I hated not being there, but with all the distractions I forgot about it pretty quickly.

It felt like no time before we were preparing for the Miami Dolphins to open the regular season. I was still in a tizzy. Just eight months ago I'd been playing the likes of Cal Poly-Pomona in front of eight thousand fans, and now I was getting ready for the Dolphins in front of sixty thousand people. I was excited just to stand on the sidelines.

It was a hot, humid autumn day in St. Louis when we entertained Miami. During the preseason you see a lot of rookies and free agents play, but when the regular season opens, many of the same old veterans are in there. It only takes a few minutes of watching to understand why. It takes special guys to play the game year after year, and while fifty to a hundred extra players try out with each team every season, only five or ten at the most ever make it. The game is played at violent speeds, much faster than the college game, and the collisions—from the sidelines—sound like car wrecks. I watched Don Shula, the Dolphins' legendary head coach, shouting from across the field. Like a kid, I was mesmerized by the sights, colors, and sounds. Carrying a clipboard and charting plays, I carefully watched Jim Hart. If you had to say one thing about Hart, it would be that he has poise. Rarely does he get rattled, or even disturbed.

"Jim, I think we can get something across the middle," he told Hanifan after the first couple series. Intensity blazed in Hart's eyes as he stared at the field. Though I felt I could play on this level, it was obvious I lacked the field leadership this man had cultivated over a sixteen-year career. Hanifan nodded his head, suggesting several pass plays to exploit Miami's typically conservative zone defense. We got the ball back, and Hart turned to go in. "Get 'em, Jimmy," I encouraged. He didn't acknowledge me.

Dropping to throw on third and long, Jim ducked under one player, but two more sandwiched him—Doug Betters, Miami's lightning-fast defensive end, hit him low, and Vern Den Herder, another pass-rush specialist, hit him high. You could hear the impact of plastic and flesh, and Jim grunted as he was slammed to the turf. He didn't get up.

"Oh, crap," Hanifan swore as trainers ran on to help the injured veteran. I was in a daze; déjà vu, just like Portland State. "Don't just stand there, Lomax," Hanifan yelled. "Warm up, kid. Move." I tossed down the clipboard, snapped my helmet on, and found a couple of extra receivers to warm up with behind the bench. Jim, whose knee was seriously bruised, was helped off the field. Before I knew it, I was in the game. For real.

For the veterans, going from Jim Hart to me in the huddle must've been like changing channels from 60 Minutes to MTV. We were radically different. His style was slow, methodical, but firm, while I was still herky-jerky, excited, loud, and boisterous. "All right, all right," I said. "Let's try to get something quick." The veterans were unimpressed. "Call the play, rookie," ordered veteran right guard Joe Bostic. I looked around, obviously displeased. But I quickly called a play—a medium-range pass.

The thrill of looking over the line of scrimmage for the first time in a real NFL game is something no quarterback ever forgets. For several seconds, as I barked the signals, the Miami defense seemed suspended in time. Here were guys I'd idolized for years, and now they were merely this week's opponents. My dream ended quickly however. I dropped to throw and took a quick look into Miami's "41–46" zone defense. Mark Bell was the primary receiver, and I watched him cut a course through several defenders. He was running a four pattern, which is an 18-yard crossing pattern, and I was anticipating his breaking free. I thought about my drop, which was a perfect 9 yards. I squared up, measured Mark, and unleashed a 40-yarder into the hole in the far corner of the zone defense. In that brief portion of a second as I was releasing the ball, I brimmed with excitement at the thought of the crowd's wild reaction when the pass was completed. In my ecstasy, I failed to notice that Mark had stumbled, making his break a little slowly and that the strong safety had come free and was moving into the flat next to Mark. The ball whizzed by Mark, one step out of reach. My head screamed, *No!*—but the strong safety disobeyed. With a Chesire-cat grin on his face, Lyle Blackwood, Miami's cagey defensive back, took the pass right in the chest. Thus I made my first-ever NFL completion to the wrong team.

But I bounced back quickly from adversity, despite the fact we were without wide receiver Mel Gray and tight end Doug Marsh. In three quarters, I completed fourteen of thirty passes for 151 yards. Preseason had been nothing like this. Never in my life had I seen guys that big moving that fast. Nothing's scarier than to glance over your shoulder and see a man who stands six-four and weighs 260 pounds, running full speed and lowering his head with the intention of removing *your* head from your body. Old habits are hard to break, and whenever I got in trouble I rolled out, twisted, and turned—anything to avoid the sack. While the fans were certainly entertained, it was proof of my lack of discipline to stay in the pocket. In essence, I was running for my life. Late in the game Doug Betters was breathing down my neck and I was running like a coyote. At the last second, he caught me, and I was falling to the ground when I unloaded a pinpoint pass to Stump Mitchell, who was about 10 yards away. The fans had never seen Jim Hart do that, and Stump was so shocked he nearly dropped the ball. Instead, it was our biggest gain of the day—about 30 yards. I think everyone had underestimated my strength, but to thread the needle while falling down, with a defensive end wrapped around you, can certainly dispel any doubts. Still, the Dolphins worked me over, sacked me three times, and constantly harassed me. We lost 20-7, but overall, I felt pretty good. At the worst, it was a lot of fun just being out there.

It was evident by Monday that Jim would be unable to play against Dallas, so Coach Hanifan named me the starter against the Cowboys, which meant I would practice the entire week as the number one quarterback. Against Miami I had just been thrown in there, but against Dallas, I had a chance to prepare myself.

NFL teams do more preparing than is done for any other professional sport. Baseball players pretty much know their opponents, but they seldom practice for any particular team. They just practice and go out and play. Pro basketball is the same. Sure, every team has its big-name guy who has to be stopped, but in no other sport is an entire week spent preparing for one opponent.

A lot of things take place during the week, and I got a crash course the week of the Dallas game. Coaches have charts from previous games that rate strengths and weaknesses for each team. Certain players are pinpointed as pivotal players; guys who can single-handedly turn a game around. For instance, the guy who would have to block the Cowboys' incredible defensive tackle, Randy White, would really be worked over in practice that week in preparation for trying to neutralize White. Each day the defense would spend several hours imitating the Dallas defense while I took snap after snap, learning to anticipate what I might see. A lot of it is guesswork. It's like a giant chess game. Our coaches were taking educated guesses as to how Dallas would play us, based on the Cowboys' previous tendencies. Meanwhile, in Dallas, the Cowboys were mapping their game plan in the same way against us. So every coach tries to add a new wrinkle or two in every game, just to give the other coaches something they haven't seen.

The classroom work was equally as hard. By watching game film of previous Dallas games, I was able to pick up tendencies, or keys, which might tip off which defense they were in. For example, there was a certain cornerback (I won't name the team), who

would always line up with his left foot back when they were playing man-to-man defense. When they were playing zone, he'd start
with his right foot back. By noticing these things on film during
the week, the quarterback can exploit them on Sunday afternoon.
But it can work both ways. Doug Williams, when he was playing
quarterback for the Tampa Bay Buccaneers, had problems during
the 1979 season. During one game it seemed the defense knew
every time it was a running play and every time it was a passing
play. Coaches were going crazy trying to figure out who or how
the plays were being given away. Suddenly, a Tampa scout, looking down with binoculars from the press box four stories above
the field, discovered the mistake: Every time it was a running
play, Williams wouldn't fasten his chin strap. On passing plays,
knowing he was taking a chance of being hit, Williams would
buckle up. The defense had been having a field day. So coaches
work hard to mask anything that might indicate the intentions of
the offense.

Forming a unique game plan for each week is where the preparation begins. Coaches scribble Xs and Os on the blackboard, and
they are translated into activities each player has seen or heard in
some form before. Yet, in some way, each game plan is unique. By
watching game films, coaches spot reaction and overreaction,
making careful notes on how individual opponents might best be
taken advantage of. Careful homework results in taking the same
basic offense each week, but adapting it in ways to deal with what
the opponent is doing. The game plan is started on Monday
night, and by Tuesday, which is the players' day off, the coaches
have it pretty well formulated. By Wednesday, it should be finished. But coaches are always adding, subtracting, making a
change here, a change there, tinkering with the offense like a
fine-tuned racing machine. But a coach never changes the basics
of the offense. Once you put an offense in during training camp,
you stay with it for the season. There simply isn't time to change
an offense in midseason. You use what you've started with and
build on it. Maybe a team will add three or four plays for a specific opponent, but it will never start from scratch.

Jim Hanifan believed in building with the running game. We

would start out with a basic package of running plays and choose
the ones that would work best against that week's opponent, according to the coaches' estimations. Then Jim, along with Harry
Gilmer, would add three or four big-play passes, along with a
combination of possession passes or plays intended just to complete short passes and maintain possession of the football. Really,
no matter who you're playing, you have a basic passing game just
like your running game. Each game, Hanifan believed in so many
passes to the tight end, so many to the strongside end, so many to
the weakside end, and so many to the running backs. It was all
patterned.

After we installed the basic running game and the basic passing
game, we would make a few adjustments here and there. An adjustment, for instance, might be just to run more toward a team's
weakness, instead of into its strength. Instead of running right at
Randy White, perhaps the best defensive tackle in the game, we
would run to the other side. Since Randy White is so quick, we
would take advantage of his quickness with a few trap or counter-
plays here and there; the play would appear to go one way, and
when he would start his pursuit, one of our offensive linemen
would come from his blindside and try to put his lights out.

Finally, coaches add a few deceptive plays for every game,
plays like screens or draws. Then maybe an onside kick or fake
field goal or fake punt would be included in the final preparations, although these were seldom used. When you use trick
plays, or "gadget" plays, you're taking a big risk; if they backfire,
your opponent can quickly score.

But the best game plan in the world is no better than the players who must execute it. Which is why the best teams have a bal-
anced mixture of brains and brawn. Nobody can get by in the
NFL with just one of the two, especially on offense. You may
have an offensive tackle with an IQ of 300, but if he isn't strong
enough to pass block, or run block, then he isn't worth a darn.
Likewise, a guy may be six-six, 280 pounds, and a perfect physical
specimen. But if he has bricks for brains, his size won't do anything but get in the way. So obviously, the coaches' hardest job is

getting the players ready to play. They have to work on the physical part just as hard as on the mental.

I had taken a projector home, and the click . . . whirr, click . . . whirr of the slow-motion action accompanied me late into the night. Watch the defense, back it up, watch it again. Reverse, forward. Click, whirr. Tom Landry's team always seemed to prefer finesse to force. Although they had some real monsters who could knock your jock off, they spent more time trying to trick you, trying to exploit you. The Cowboys will give you *fake* keys, just to throw you off. They want you to hesitate for a second, to think you're seeing something that you're not. If you fall for that, you may be trying to identify something that is irrelevant to the play, which destroys the essence of the play itself. There is no way a rookie can absorb all the possibilities. Occasionally a rookie quarterback will excel, but it's usually by accident. As I prepared for the Dallas Cowboys, I was unaware of how or when all these coverages, blitzes, and countless formations would finally make sense. I just kept studying, knowing somehow it all would eventually come together.

Warming up against Dallas was a thrill. I stared at the stupid hole in the roof. Texas Stadium is domed, with the exception of a big hole that allows just enough sunlight to cast weird shadows and piercing sunlight in various patches all over the field. I really felt in charge, but I still had a few butterflies flittering around in my stomach. I felt good after the game started and just tried to settle down and go to work. The funny thing, though, was that all the preparation I'd done for the game flew out the window. When I walked up to the line of scrimmage for the first play of the game, I saw a menacing Charlie Waters, the Cowboys' perennial All-Pro defensive back, staring at me with piercing eyes. I gave him a confident wink, which forced him to smile and shake his head. "I really got off on that," he told me afterward. "You're awful brave for such a young kid."

I spent the afternoon running around like a chicken with its

head cut off. Announcers were calling me the second coming of
the scrambling Fran Tarkenton, which wasn't true. Fran knew
what he was doing. My scrambling was a combination of being a
rookie, not really being sure of what was happening around me,
and being scared. On one play Charlie Waters blitzed, and I
never saw him. In fact, I had no idea what defense they were in. I
was just taking snaps, running around, and trying to make something happen. Charlie came pouring in out of nowhere and had
me by the back of my jersey. I jerked away, circled around the
other way, and amid all the confusion caught a glimpse of half-
back Willard Harrell running downfield. Terrified, I let it go in
Willard's general direction. Amazingly, he caught it in stride for a
60-yard touchdown. The Dallas fans were going wild watching
the rabbit hunt, which went on all day. Another bomb fell in the
arms of defensive back-wide receiver Roy Green for 62 yards. We
lost, 30-17, but the coaches were pretty impressed with my 295-
yard performance.

Hanifan approached my locker afterward. "Hey, kid," he said.
"You looked pretty good. If you can play that well now, imagine
how good you'll be when you have some idea of what the heck is
going on out there." I laughed. My scrambling technique was
only temporary. The biggest difference between Fran Tarkenton
and myself was something he is quick to tell all young quarterbacks: You need *patience*. The press loved my scrambling style,
and they began writing about how immobile Jim Hart was and
how dazzling I was. Which proves how little the media or fans
know about what takes place on the field. Scrambling out of
fright sometimes allows big plays to happen, but more often than
not it disrupts the flow of the offense. It's hit-and-miss opportunities and a lack of understanding. Fran has really been the only
true successful "organized" scrambler in the NFL. But few have
the cunning dipsy-do moves of Tarkenton. I was merely improvising while I learned to maintain my composure. My biggest
problem was trying to keep the Xs and Os where they had been
drawn on the blackboard. It's easy for a coach to diagram Charlie
Waters or Lyle Blackwood with a simple X in chalk. When
you're looking into his eyes, it's not quite so simple anymore. The

human element is what makes professional football so exciting. And, as Fran once said, I had to learn to avoid forcing things. While my scrambling was thrilling the crowds, I would be far better off to learn first what the defense was trying to do, then respond. The trick was being patient enough to find that path.

Hart returned after the Dallas game, and, except for occasional mopping-up performances in the fourth quarter, I saw little action for the next two months. While every quarterback wants to play, I was still enjoying my role of standing on the sidelines and really studying the professional game. I was so absorbed in my new life-style that I was neglecting friends and relatives. With all the things to do and see in St. Louis there just didn't seem to be enough time in one day. My rookie year I lived in a house with two other teammates: Ron Coder, a big guard from Penn State and a devout Christian; and Don Schwartz, a rookie defensive back from Washington State. We were all new to St. Louis, and it seemed there was constantly something we wanted to do. The opportunities for young players are endless.

St. Louis extends along the Mississippi River and is really a beautiful city when the sun is shining. Though the humidity is terrible, there are few things prettier to see than the sun sparkling off the Gateway Arch, the nation's tallest monument. The historic riverfront area includes the Old Courthouse, which was the site of the famous Dred Scott slavery trial. Busch Stadium, our home turf, is located just a few blocks from the river in the downtown area. The residential area of St. Louis, however, is spread outward from the downtown area.

Thus free time was spent exploring our new home, and it was hard to find time for everybody. Feeling like the new guy on the block, I quickly tried to be friendly to a lot of people. Very visible in the media, I found it hard to go to dinner without being spotted by someone with a camera. Girls suddenly gave me more attention than ever. I took advantage of my image. Which was why I preferred to date out of the city; I didn't want to become known as a womanizer. Though I never entertained "easy" girls, and avoided the dopers and hookers entirely, most of the girls I dated just didn't interest me. Most of my dates were just a movie here, dinner there, and I seldom saw the same girl more than once or twice.

My vision had become centered on my career, and though I could sense problems were developing, I couldn't stop it. I was really caught up in the fast-paced life-style. Once we got into the season, I was no longer homesick. Trying hard to fit in with the veterans, coaches, and the organization, I would often go home at night and just fall into bed utterly exhausted. Because of my hectic schedule, I really neglected my folks, Stuart, and most of the people back home.

Occasionally Ron Kincaid would call. He was loving his new role as pastor at Sunset Presbyterian, but he never sermonized over the phone. Most of our discussions were just friendly chit-chat sessions, although Ron would very smoothly interject a note about my prayer life here and there.

"Neil, you know we're praying for you," he'd say. "What prayer requests do you have? What have you been praying about lately?"

Ron never forgot me. Nor did he ever question me about drugs or other problems common among young professional athletes. All he cared about was letting me know he loved me as a Christian brother. That meant a great deal to me.

My daily devotions really helped keep me close to Christ during that first year. If you're too busy for God, you're too busy, and I followed a daily devotional program that forced me to spend some quiet time with Jesus every day. Unfortunately, I was too nearsighted to pray for spiritual growth; instead, I was praying for my health, for God to help me overcome my nervousness, to help me be popular, to help me throw the ball better. Never did I pray to be the starting quarterback, but my number-one concern should have been my spiritual health. Everything was moving so fast, my mind was constantly in a tailspin. It's easy to criticize the dilemmas some young men in that situation get into, but unless a person has been through it, it's impossible to understand. Without the Lord, the big salary, the sudden popularity, and the macho image can be a dangerous, volatile combination.

The local Fellowship of Christian Athletes chapter, which included a team bible study, met once a week, and I was an active participant. Several veterans, like Pat Tilley and Jim Hart, also were regulars at the meetings. Walt Enoch, a businesslike man in his late fifties, was the director. It was easy to see he had a calling for such a ministry. Lovable, pleasant, and fatherly, he cared about the players as individuals, not as professional athletes. He was quick to lend both ears whenever someone needed to talk.

While I was spending my time trying to adapt to the rush of new experiences and tending to my new career, my family was getting downright upset over my lack of communication. My financial situation, in particular, had become an issue with my parents. They had expected to see some extra cash a little sooner. I'd bought my dad the 1977 Citation he'd asked for, but Mom was not bashful about telling friends and relatives that she hoped I'd lay out cash to buy them a new home. My salary had been reported in the papers, and though it wasn't much in big-league terms, it was more than enough to cause deep waves of reaction in Lake Oswego. Too often people wrongly assume that having such cash flow solves everything, because most people perceive money as the answer to all problems. Being frugal with money, in my case, has led to accusations of my cheapness, stinginess, and lack of concern.

Misunderstanding of my motives led to hurt feelings in my family. Mitch spoke candidly of the differences between what each member of the family—my parents in particular—anticipated as a result of my income. They "expected to see some of the cash," but got the "trickle-down effect" instead, as Mitch puts it.

I received a letter from my parents midway through my rookie season telling me flat out that "your money has divided the family." They insisted I had made financial agreements that I couldn't remember. I steadfastly refused to go overboard on what I spent on my family, simply because the dollar signs, in my opinion, were taking their eyes off God as their source of supply. Since guys like Earl Campbell were buying their parents homes and cars, my decision was met with some bitterness.

In retrospect, I was kind of a jerk about the situation. Mitch feels I could've changed everything just by sharing more of my thoughts with Mom and Dad. They associated not receiving monetary gifts with the idea that they were losing their son, according to Mitch. Which is why, today, I regret not having given them more time and attention during that period. That was a mistake on my part. There just seemed to be so many demands on my time. Yet parents can't be replaced. Perhaps, if I'd been a little more tender, a little more sensitive to their thoughts, the issue might not have been blown out of proportion. My fame was affecting my parents in a hard way. They were caught up in the glory, but finding the pressure tough to cope with. They wanted very much to be associated with me, and since I failed to give them time, they created their own avenues. They subscribed to the *St. Louis Post-Dispatch*, wore St. Louis Cardinals attire, and continued hanging action pictures of me all over the house.

On November 8, 1981, we lost our seventh game of the year when Philadelphia just shellacked us, 52-10, before our home crowd. They beat us about every way a team can be beat. We slipped to 3-7, and the fans and media were putting Coach Hanifan under intense pressure to give me more game experience, especially since the season appeared to be a lost cause. When I found a message on Wednesday morning, November 11, to see Coach Hanifan in his office, I had a good idea of what was about to transpire.

Coach Hanifan's office was a tiny room located in the rear of a larger room, which housed the desks of the rest of the coaching staff. Pictures of his family and football memorabilia adorned one wall. On the far wall, a huge depth chart, with each player's name stuck under various positions, took up most of the available

space. A projector, from which a dog-eared reel of film was hanging, sat on his desk, facing a yellowed screen that hung on another wall. On one side of the room was a couch where Hanifan
had collapsed from exhaustion many nights during the season
after working into the morning hours. A cluttered, cheap-looking
Naugahyde chair sat on his right. On his desk, which was a mass
of papers, charts, and computer printouts, were two ashtrays, full
of Vantage cigarette butts.

I pushed a newspaper aside and sat down on the chair. Slowly
and deliberately, Coach Hanifan jerked another cigarette from
the dwindling pack—already his second of the day—and lit up,
taking a drag that seemed to last forever.

"Neil," he huffed, blowing pale blue smoke across the room in
a giant cloud. "We're gonna make a little change." He tossed the
cigarette pack on his desk, reclined in his chair, and sucked hard
again on the cancer stick. I was getting impatient. "We're making
a change in the offense, and that change is primarily you."

I nodded anxiously. My throat and eyes burned as his cloud of
smoke finally engulfed me as he continued.

"You're gonna start. How's that sound to you?"

I wasn't too surprised, but still I didn't really know what to say.
Coach Hanifan and Jim Hart had been pretty close over the last
few years, and I knew it was a tough and emotional decision for
him to make. But I pondered the fact that maybe the pressure
from the fans and media, and possibly Mr. Bidwill, had led to his
decision.

I nodded. After walking far enough away from his office to be
out of earshot, I let out a whoop of excitement.

My teammates greeted the new situation with mixed feelings.
"It wasn't all Hart's fault," Dan Dierdorf kept telling the local
media. "The whole team is guilty." Hart turned very bitter, very
calloused over the whole issue. His attitude toward me became
even worse than it had been. That week in practice was quite
awkward; you can't just walk out and tell the linemen and receiv-

ers and everybody else, "Hey, I'm the starting quarterback now
. . . you better start blocking and catching. . . ." You've got to
show them. It's just like Christianity; quit talking and start walking. Leadership and respect are earned.

Pat Tilley came to mean a great deal to me during this time.
He and Jim Hart had been very close, but as a Christian, Pat was
nursing me through this transition period. Even still, he showed
support for Jim, but was fair in his statements to the media about
the situation. "Jim doesn't deserve all the blame," he would say.
My first encounter with Pat had been in a mini-camp, when he
invited me to a Bible study. Later that night we had dinner and
saw a movie together, and I knew instantly we would become
friends.

Lively and colorful, Pat has qualities that just reach out and
grab you. Watching Pat during the year also really taught me
what it means to be a true husband and father. His wife, Diane,
and his children are the focal point of his life outside of Christ. In
fact, I set their relationship as a standard for my marriage. His
Christian love and selflessness during such a tough time spoke
louder than words.

In my first start against Buffalo, running back O. J. Anderson
pounded out 171 yards rushing and was simply unstoppable. The
defense was equally pounding, and I was about average. We
blanked the hapless Bills, 24-0. I came down with strep
throat the next week during preparations for Baltimore and
missed two days of practice. Once the game started, however, all
pains were put aside. Pat Tilley was on fire, and we connected on
the longest pass of his career—a 75-yard pass down the sideline.
Pat is a vanishing breed among NFL receivers. His short stature
and "slow" 4.6 speed are considered inadequate by most coaches,
but it's tough to measure a guy's heart. "A lot of people say you
need speed at wide receiver," Pat told me after his incredible
catch. "But you can have all the speed in the world and not get
open. I know how to get open." He was right. With Pat, tight

end Doug Marsh, and Roy Green, who was really coming alive, we were unstoppable. We beat the Colts, 35-24, and I tallied 219 yards.

A week later we were introduced to partisan boos in Foxboro, Massachusetts, as we went to war with the New England Patriots. We quickly warmed up the frigid air, and Roy Green and I dominated the Pats' secondary. New England knotted the score at 20-20 with less than two minutes to play, and the pressure rose with the roar of the crowd. Minutes later, I faked a handoff to O. J. on the right-hand side and bootlegged to the left, but their veteran defensive end, Julius Adams, poured through, grabbed my jersey, and started dragging me to the ground. Improvising, as always, I curled away from Adams, and the entire back of my jersey ripped off. He was holding it in his hands as the Patriots coaches screamed that I was down. I sprinted away from two other defenders, then spotted O. J. all alone in the right flat. I tossed it to him and he carried it about 40 yards. The Patriots coaching staff was penalized 15 yards for unsportsmanlike conduct, and presto, we were in a position to win it.

"Okay, guys, we can win this thing," I said in the huddle. I could sense a newfound confidence in my teammates. I was slowly becoming their leader. "Eight fake zero-four shoot two." The play was designed to go to Roy, who would fake across the middle but then burst back outside. Bingo. Roy ran a great route, I threw an average pass just a little behind him, and he made a fantastic catch. One defender slipped and Roy outran the other one for a touchdown. I was going wild on the sidelines. I didn't feel like a rookie anymore; I finished twenty of twenty-eight for 280 yards. The late comeback was the confidence-builder I needed to prove to myself I could play in this league.

The drive in the last two minutes will always stick in my mind. We did it as a team. I was not a rookie then; I truly became their quarterback. The next week we bombed New Orleans, 30-3, before a huge crowd at Busch Stadium. Four starts, four victories, and I had become the talk of the town. I quit apologizing for taking Jim Hart's job. But it was unfair to Jim; suddenly, everyone was writing him off. Jim had given sixteen years of his life to the St. Louis organization, and overnight, nobody cared about him anymore. I could've run for mayor at that point and won easily, although I did wonder if maybe, some sixteen years down the road, the fans would be treating me like that.

But I couldn't hide my boyish excitement. One day, we're 3-7, and then suddenly, the play-offs are a possibility.

Mitch, then in his second year at Trinity Evangelical Divinity School in Chicago, came down a few days before the New York Giants game, and I arranged for him to speak at our chapel service prior to the contest.

Seeing Mitch again was great. He was still his quiet, humble, mature self. Mitch has insight beyond his years. During conversations he often stares into space, listening, pondering, and then calculating answers that usually are right on the money. His soft voice is never offensive, and his mannerisms set a perfect example of the way a Christian should act. During his visit, he provided a much-needed spiritual example without having to say anything.

He was a little nervous around the players, but he was excited to have the kind of access to an NFL team that only a football-playing brother could provide. He spent a great deal of time with me, watching all my preparations for the New York Giants, who promised to be a stiff test. The day of the game I took him to pre-game meal with me early in the morning at the hotel.

"These guys are huge, Neil," he kept saying quietly, panning the room. "I can't believe I'm going to teach them anything. I hope I don't make any of these behemoths mad at me." He was so nervous about speaking in front of them he couldn't eat; instead, he sipped orange juice. My teammates and I weren't so shy. Pounds and pounds of bacon, eggs, steaks, toast, and other well-cooked breakfast goods disappeared quickly from the buffet table.

Chapel was shortly after breakfast, and a "crowd" of about sixteen players was present when we came in. The atmosphere was deadly quiet and extremely tense. Football players before a big game are quite similar to soldiers prior to battle; the tension is so thick it knots your stomach and grips your throat. I had told Coach Hanifan my brother was speaking in chapel, but I was still floored when he ducked inside and sat down in the back row. That was the only service I ever saw him come to. I found it tough to keep my mind on God during chapel; I couldn't get the first series of plays out of my mind, and Satan tormented me with thoughts of the New York defense as Mitch rose to speak. It's hard to think about Christ with "Scat 66 Flare" on your mind. But when Mitch began to speak, I sensed the Lord taking control of my thoughts.

"God has laid on my heart to share with you guys the parable about men who honor themselves," Mitch said. He cleared his throat and took control of the situation. What he had to say wasn't easy. "Sometimes as professional athletes, it's easy to let people exalt you, and we approach situations with great pride and we lack humility."

Wow. Mitch always was direct. But he didn't stop there.

"When I was in high school, I gained my fame through being a rally team member, a cheerleader, and through my dancing. But as I developed physically after my graduation, I became a pretty good basketball player. So when people would ask me where I played, I'd say, Lake Oswego High School.

"One day I was playing pickup basketball at Portland State, and I was playing some pretty good hoops. I really felt cocky. Then somebody asked, 'Hey, where did you play in high school?' I gave an arrogant smirk: 'Lake Oswego High,' I told him. The guy stared at me for several seconds, and then blurted, 'Naw, man. You . . . you're the *rally* guy!' Never was I more embarrassed in my life.

"Let others exalt you," Mitch insisted. "Don't exalt yourself. Approach every situation with great humility. Be humble; pride is the original sin. Approach situations with the mind of Christ. Would Christ be arrogant? Cocky? Would Christ exalt Himself? Pride goeth before a fall."

When Mitch finished, there was dead silence. When we filed

out, my eyes caught Jim Hart's. For several seconds, I returned his glare. He turned away.

All season I'd heard about Lawrence Taylor, the Giants' great rookie linebacker. When I looked across the line at him, I'd never seen such intensity in my life. The Giants' game plan was to negate my scrambling ability by putting on a fierce outside pass rush that forced me back into the pocket, where there was even more heat. It worked, to say the least. I was seeing more white jerseys and blue helmets than anything else, and every passing down I was getting smeared.

We were tied at 10-all late in the second quarter when I dropped to throw. Taylor blitzed, and just wiped out our rookie tight end Greg LaFleur. I never saw him. I thought I had Tilley open over the middle and was in the process of throwing the ball when the lights went out. I heard my back and shoulder give an ugly pop as he drove his helmet in at full speed; my head whiplashed violently backward. The ball skittered out of my hand, and L. T. drove me facedown into the turf, with a full-body slam. Doug Martin, a defensive end, picked up the fumble and ran it in for a touchdown. I was fading in and out of reality. Taylor is a tremendous athlete, and he can knock you into tomorrow.

I regained my senses, but not before Jim Hart had to play several series while I recuperated. When I went back in, the Giants continued their onslaught. Defensive tackle Gary Jeter came gushing in from somewhere in the third quarter, and, bam, I was out again. My memory is sketchy about everything that happened. All I know is we lost, 20-10, and I had a whale of a headache afterwards.

The locker room was deadly quiet. My body felt like I'd been dragged underneath a truck for several miles. For four games in a row it had been a piece of cake, but in a matter of three hours I realized how tough you had to be to play in this league. All the excitement had come to a screeching halt. Limping back from

the showers, I slumped in front of my locker. Ouch. I hope the
Lord quits using Lawrence Taylor to reduce my pride.

The Giants knocked us out of the play-off contention. The
next week against Super Bowl-bound Philadelphia it was obvious
our guys didn't even want to play. They just wanted to get
the season over with. It was very cold, the rug was hard, and nobody cared. My arms were scraped from one end to the other
from the turf, and I spent most of the game on my back. I threw
three interceptions and gave up 57 yards on seven head-pound-
ing sacks as the Eagles whipped us, 38-0, to end the long, long
season.

I was cleaning out my locker in Busch Stadium the next Monday when John Sonderegger, a Cardinals beat writer from the *St.
Louis Post-Dispatch* swung by. "Hey, John," I said, packing my
bags and sorting through leftover items. The bearded, burly
scribe, whose stories are usually factual and frank, came over and
sat down. "Tough game," he said, staring at the scrapes and
bruises on my arms.

"You should've been on the field, " I grinned.

"Mind if I get a few things?" he asked, taking out a note pad. I
shook my head. "How will you feel if Hart doesn't return?" he
asked.

I smiled. You have to watch reporters. John's a good guy, but
it's his job to come back with a story. And that, to me, was a
loaded question. "John, I won't touch that one." He didn't seem
too surprised, but instead was prepared with another verbal
projectile: "Do you think Hart will be satisfied sitting behind you
next season, kind of the way Bob Griese finished his career in
Miami as a backup to David Woodley?"

In essence, that was the same question, just reloaded. Relentless guys, these reporters.

"To be perfectly honest, no," I told him, slinging an old,
smelly sock into a garbage can. "Jim is a competitor, and he
wants to play. I don't see it as a problem between me and Jim. It's

between Hart and the management and the coaches. That's where the problem lies."

I figured there wasn't any sense in backing down. The team went 4-2 with me at quarterback, and I had really gained confidence during my first year. I knew now I could play with the big boys, and I wasn't going to let the Philadelphia game leave a bad taste in my mouth. One thing was clear, however: I couldn't do it alone. The Giants and Eagles proved that. But I knew I could drop back in the pocket, stay poised, and read coverages against NFL defenses. And whether Hart wanted to believe it or not, his days as the starting quarterback were over.

I took a red-eye flight back to Portland that night. It was Monday, December 21, 1981. I'd be home for Christmas. I was relieved the season had ended. My rookie season felt like six years, not six months. I had learned and experienced so many things. I thought of Portland, my parents, my friends, and Portland State. I was hoping to wrap up my degree in Speech Communications/Journalism at PSU during the spring semester. I was beaten, battered, and tired. *I'll be back*, I thought, as the lights of St. Louis disappeared far behind me in the darkness below. Next year, I'd be the confident veteran.

Sighing deeply, I stared out the window into space, wondering what the immediate future held for me. I couldn't wait to get home.

9

Visions of Love, London, and Labor Disputes

"Controversy equalizes fools and wise men—and the fools know it."

—Oliver Wendell Holmes, Jr.

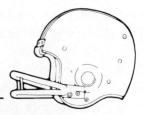

In March 1982 I went down to Portland's KOIN television station for an interview. I was standing in the hallway talking to an anchorman when I noticed a cute brunette bustling about, taking scripts of that evening's newscast around to each anchor in the newsroom. She was gorgeous. Tall and lean with beautiful brown eyes, she had an aloof appeal. Several times we caught each other staring from across the room, and I smiled to myself, half-embarrassed. I finished talking and turned to leave through a glass door. Suddenly, this girl came down the hall, and we met face to face. "Hi," I said, smiling as we passed. She grinned broadly.

I was using the spring semester to finish up my degree at Portland State and spending the majority of my time trying to graduate before summer—and my second pro season—arrived. I had forgotten about the girl at the TV station until the next day while walking down the dim hallways to my next class at PSU. Behind me I could hear heels clicking on the tile floors. My curiosity got the best of me and I peeked over my shoulder. I was stunned. It was *her*, the knockout from the television station. Never one to run from an awkward situation, I wheeled around.

"Haven't I seen you somewhere before?" I blurted, suddenly realizing the line I'd innocently given her. She started laughing. I adjusted my baseball hat nervously. "That was pretty original," she replied, flashing a smile. "But yes, you have seen me before. At the station, remember?" I tried not to stare. "Remember?" "How could I forget?" We both chuckled. "What's your name?"

"Laurie Exley," she said. *Laurie. What a cute name*, I thought. "Well Laurie, my name's Neil. Neil Lomax." I waited for the usual reaction, but she gave no sign of recognition. We talked some more, namely about *her* career. That was a switch. She was finishing her degree in history while working at the TV station. Finally, she asked me what I did for a living. This was my big chance to make an impression. "Well, I'm a quarterback for the St. Louis Cardinals in the NFL," I said, making a throwing motion with my arm. "You know, a quarterback, the guy who throws the ball."

"I *know* what a quarterback is," she replied airily, eyes twinkling. "I'm not stupid." Turning, she continued down the hall, heels clicking. Ahem.

A week later, on the last day of finals, I saw her standing in the cafeteria line at school, and I ran up to her. We chitchatted for a few minutes, and then I got to the point. "What are you doing after finals?" I asked. "I've planned to go check out Arizona State in Tempe," she said. "I hear they have a good TV journalism program, and I'm thinking about transferring over there."

"What a coincidence," I answered, smiling. "I'm going to Tempe, too, to visit John Mistler, a good friend I met in a college all-star game. Hey, I've got an idea." I reached into my notebook, tore out a piece of paper, and scribbled down John's phone number. "When you get there, you call me at John's house," I instructed. "Call me and we'll do something." She looked kind of hesitant, but agreed. "I'll try," she said.

I had informed Anne, John's wife, that a girl from Portland might be calling and to be sure and get a message if she did. But for two agonizing and embarrassing days, the phone never rang. "Yeah, Neil," Anne joked. "You must've really charmed this girl!" When I had just about given up hope, she called on the third day, much to my relief. We dated the last three nights she was in Arizona, and when we got back to Portland, we started dating pretty regularly. There was something special, something mystical to me about this girl, but I still couldn't pinpoint the feeling. Rather, I just enjoyed her company and we ended up having a fabulous spring and summer together. Time passed quickly and I was soon on my way back to training camp and St. Louis, my home away from home.

I had picked up a copy of *Sport* magazine to accompany me on the flight to St. Louis. Flipping through football previews and predictions, I came across a story by senior editor Peter Griffin which left a lump in my throat. The article described the 1981 season as "a garden party conducted under a darkening sky . . . management-labor negotiations are pointing toward a player strike." During the off-season, I had been aware that both sides were far apart, but I had passed off the possibility of an actual walkout by our union, the National Football League Players Association. But this article said differently, and supported that contention with facts. The basic collective bargaining agreement between NFL owners and players, which had been signed in

1977, had expired. Issues of priority included contributions to the player pension fund, pre- and postseason pay, safety, and insurance. But the most difficult issue was free agency, and what we players might want in its place.

There was a lot of talk—then and now—about free agency, and clearly, the current system didn't appear to be working. In February 1981, 137 NFL players became free agents, enabling them to negotiate with any team that wanted to make an offer. Only one, Bob Young of Houston, received an official offer. Nobody else got a bid. Not Walter Payton. Not Lynn Swann. Free agency in the NFL is not like free agency in baseball or basketball. Players and owners agree that is a big reason why salaries in the NFL are well below those in the other two sports. Some players that year, like Vince Ferragamo, Billy (White Shoes) Johnson, and James Scott, had already jumped leagues for better contracts in the Canadian Football League. That was scary. Ironically, in the four years that the free-agent system had been in effect in football, one player out of an eligible 447 had changed teams as a free agent. That was Norm Thompson, a defensive back out of Utah who had played for none other than the St. Louis Cardinals. He signed with the Colts in 1977, but was out of football by 1978.

The controversy surrounding free agency involved compensation, or what a team would have to give up in order to acquire a player who had belonged to another club. For instance, if a player with at least four years in the NFL became a free agent after his contract expired, any team that acquired him would have to compensate the team he left with a college draft choice. And that draft choice would have to range from a third-round pick to two consecutive-year, first-round picks; it was based on the size of the contract the free agent signed. By now I was vividly aware of the value the NFL placed on first-round draft picks, which explained why few players were deemed worth *two* such previous jewels.

The article pointed out that the dispute also centered on players' salaries, which were low compared to salaries in other sports. The average salary at that time in the NBA was $185,000; in major league baseball, $172,000; in the National Hockey League, $108,000. In the NFL, the average salary in 1981 had been $79,000, far below our cousins in other professional sports. And nowhere but in football do you pay such a physical price for playing the sport.

Griffin wrote:

> Except for Walter Payton, the highest-paid player in the league when he signed a new, three-year contract which boosted his salary in excess of $600,000, the highest-paid player in the NFL is Billy Sims, at $377,500. Only four other players make more than $300,000 a year. Earl Campbell, entering his fourth year in the league and regarded by many as the top player in the game, asked to renegotiate his contract this past off-season. He was refused. Last year he earned an even $300,000—nearly $200,000 less than Ed Farmer, a journeyman relief pitcher for the Chicago White Sox.

The story was a bad omen. Rather than directly challenge free-agency rules, the union had decided to ask for a significant and outright share of total NFL revenues, something on the order of 55 percent of gross receipts from television, ticket sales, concessions, merchandising—everything. That money would be distributed to players according to a systematic wage scale, based on years of service, the player's role as a starter or reserve, minutes played, and other factors. There would be no individual contracts under such an agreement. By the time I had stepped off the plane to attend my second training camp, several offers and counteroffers between the union and the league had been made.

Ed Garvey, then executive director of the NFLPA, had already issued an ultimatum to Jack Donlan, who represented management: either come across with a reasonable agreement, or there won't be a 1982 season.

Reading Griffin's story certainly didn't encourage me any. I was against a strike, and I felt most of the players in the league didn't know enough about the issues at stake. Players were rallying around the union without any idea of what was taking place. Many players weren't prepared financially to strike. Even more didn't realize the long-term ramifications of a strike. Like the fans, I had believed it would never happen. Suddenly, I was concerned.

I waded into training camp drills as gung ho as ever, elated to be the first-string quarterback. The rift between Jim Hart and me broadened as he came back for his seventeenth season. When Coach Hanifan told the media Hart would be utilized as a "veteran backup . . . and sideline tutor for Lomax," reporters asked Hart what kind of advice he was giving me. "It's hard to give advice to a kid who doesn't want any, to a guy who feels he doesn't need any. Neil knows it all . . . what could I possibly tell him?" Statements like that, in my opinion, showed that he couldn't accept his new role and the fact that his time had finally come, as it does for every quarterback. I hope when my time comes to leave football that God gives me the strength to accept it.

Nevertheless, I plunged ahead. Hart could say what he wanted, but the job was mine. We breezed through training camp, and a sense of togetherness began developing among the younger guys on the team. Many of us were good, and we knew it. We were beginning to think we could win every time out, like a good team should. Unlike the veterans, who had been through countless losing efforts, we were still pretty unscathed. We finished 1–3 in preseason, losing three games by a total of 28 points. Three meaningless games, in which we felt we played pretty darn well. We were never embarrassed.

The most notable events of the preseason were the union solidarity handshakes that took place prior to each game. Ed Garvey had suggested that the players take part in the thirty-second display before games to prove to management we were united in our efforts and threats to strike. I didn't like the idea, and thought it was a bunch of baloney. It was getting very complicated, but I tried to believe the union knew what it was doing. Our first solidarity handshake, at San Francisco before 51,931 fans, drew the biggest torrent of boos I've ever heard. Various objects flew from the stands as nearly two hundred veterans, rookies, and free agents ran to midfield and shook hands. Most of us were laughing; the whole idea was still a pretty big joke.

It ceased to be funny after the weekend, when Jack Donlan, executive director of the NFL management council, instructed individual teams to set fines for handshakes at one hundred dollars per player. With Donlan's encouragement, Seattle head coach Jack Patera fined all his players half their regular-season game pay for pregame handshakes. That just resulted in the players getting angrier. Now you had angry players who wanted a strike just because they had been fined. Most, however, still had no idea when, where, or why there might be a strike. Three days after Donlan's brilliant idea to fine players, the National Labor Relations Board rescinded the order.

On September 8, 1982, four days before the beginning of the regular season, management made its first contract offer, which included illegal strikebreaker bonuses of $10,000 per year, severance payment beginning in 1983, an unworkable grievance procedure, and deletion of annual pension contribution. Management rejected everything the union had proposed over the preceding six months, and Jack Donlan predicted that management would spend $1.6 billion over the next five years. Well, Garvey and Gene Upshaw, then president of the players' union, took management's proposal like a slap in the face. "In essence, they've ignored all our work and negotiations for the last six months," Upshaw said. "Two can play this game."

We opened the season at New Orleans against the Saints, and we kicked them around bad. The defense was hitting like sledgehammers, I was pretty sharp for an opening game, and the offense was clicking. I hardly had to throw the ball—completing only ten of eighteen for 92 yards and a touchdown—because O. J. and Stump were hammering it down their throats. The Saints were not considered a strong team, but any time you play in the Super Dome, it's a tough place to win, so it was a start. The next week, however, we were humbled when we ran up against our old nemesis, the Dallas Cowboys. We lost 24–7, but despite the score we stayed in it until the last. For the second straight year against Dallas, I put on a show, throwing for nearly 300 yards and our lone touchdown. If anything, I had earned the respect of their secondary. Despite the score, my confidence was high after the game. My good friend Robin Pflugrad came in with his parents to see the game, and I was really proud I had performed well. We celebrated that night in anticipation that this would be our season.

Wrong. Ed Garvey was furious with Jack Donlan over the collective bargaining agreement negotiations, and there were sessions when it appeared the two executives might come to blows. Name-calling, threatening negotiations were the norm, and the event had become a circus for national media. The nine-member executive committee of the NFLPA voted to authorize a strike on Monday, September 20, and it looked as though the inevitable would happen.

The union's request for a fixed percentage of revenue dated back to the sixties, when the NFL was competing with the American Football League for players. Then, according to the players' figures, two-thirds of the league's revenues went into player salaries. Since the two leagues had merged in 1970, the union told us, that figure had dropped to 30 percent. The owners, however, were saying that current payrolls constituted 44 percent of their revenues. The players who stood to benefit the most were linemen, kickers, and defensive backs. The so-called "glamour" guys, quarterbacks like myself, running backs, and receivers, would gain the least. The scale of minimum salaries the union was asking for was based on seniority, regardless of position. Under that proposal, all first-year guys had to make $75,000; seventh-year players $175,000; all twelfth-year players, $400,000. Players would be free to negotiate for additional money. But according to the union's figures a tenth-year quarterback would get only 5 percent more than the then average for that position, while linemen would get a 150 percent increase and kickers 290 percent.

Although the New York Giants and Green Bay Packers still

had to play that Monday night, both management and union were bracing for a strike. "The major stumbling blocks remain on the players' insistence of a fixed-wage scale," Donlan said. "The owners will not abandon the current system for the union's plan." Garvey retaliated by saying that the NFL's track record in former negotiations necessitated the guarantee. "In 1974 (the last year of negotiations), they granted us a limited free agency and said 'trust us on this, it will work,' " Garvey explained to the media. "We did, and five hundred and fifty free agents later almost nobody had received an offer from another club. This time we want the written guarantee."

The union did back down somewhat when it changed its demands from a percentage of the gross to just a percentage of television. The union also proposed a wage scale tied to a fund into which owners would pay $1.6 billion over four years. Again, the union was turned down, as Donlan said owners would never agree to a wage scale, and refused to bargain collectively over wages. It flat-out rejected tying player compensation to TV revenues, which is an incredible $14.5 million per team. Can you imagine a team grossing that much before the first ticket, parking space, or hot dog is even sold? He later said that management's offer would guarantee $1.6 billion, but he insisted that management must have discretion on how it would spend 70 percent.

This sounded pretty fair to most, but Upshaw and Garvey told him to take a hike. Then, prior to the Monday night game on September 20, it was announced that the NFLPA had signed contracts with promoters in Texas and Louisiana to begin a series of all-star games featuring NFL players selected by the players' union. The NFLPA had reached agreement with television mogul Ted Turner to broadcast the games on his cable television station. I couldn't believe it. And if anybody thought I was going to risk my career for all-star games, they were crazy.

The worst was realized when Garvey announced the NFLPA would strike after the Giants-Packers game unless a "twelfth-hour proposal" was made by management. The owners laughed it off. The Packers, behind an 11-yard touchdown run by Eddie Lee

Ivery, beat the Giants, 27–19. The game ended shortly after mid-
night, when it was announced that the fifteen hundred players of
the NFL were officially on strike.

Privately, I was furious. I wanted to play ball. The Cardinals
had gotten off to a solid start, I was finally the starting quarterback, and things were proceeding nicely. That quickly, it was all
over.

The few weeks that followed were total pandemonium. The
owners wouldn't allow striking players to use the stadium or team
facilities to work out, so we chose various other sites. Ha. We'd
get together, sling a few passes, and inevitably start horsing
around. Half the team wouldn't show, and guys would be goofing
off in no time. No one seemed serious about staying ready in case
a settlement was reached, especially as the strike wore on. More
often than not, most of the players, including myself, ended up
playing golf instead of practicing when we met for our "organized" get-togethers. Although it lowered my handicap, it was
frustrating.

I was still dating several other girls in the St. Louis area, but I
missed Laurie. That surprised me, because I really didn't know
her that well. But I missed her bad. Unbeknownst to me, Laurie
had virtually quit dating other guys and was struggling to come to
grips with a growing desire to know the Lord better. She later told
me it was my spiritual influence and that of her mother, Donna
Exley, that encouraged her to get closer to God. Occasionally, I
would surprise her with a phone call, and we both were always
excited to talk to each other. The phone calls grew more and
more frequent.

Depression started setting in as the strike ate into the season.
October came and little progress had been made. On October 18,
I received my "Update '82," an internal brochure, for players
only, which outlined the happenings of the strike. This one informed me that Sam Kagel, a seventy-three-year-old mediator

with great experience as a neutral arbitrator, had been called in to attempt to settle the dispute. The newsletter also said that:

> Some progress has been made on noneconomic issues; for example, a joint union/league drug counseling program that stresses confidentiality. There will be no spot-check urinalysis. The grievance procedure has been greatly improved, and you now will have access to your medical files. While none of these issues would have caused a strike, the negotiations committee has fought hard to gain these benefits to help you when you have a problem.

Meanwhile, I wasn't getting paid. The NFLPA had started its all-star games, and I wasn't among the all-stars, by choice. They were a huge failure; the first game, before a "crowd" of only 8,706, the NFC East team beat an AFC East team 23–22, on a 45-yard field goal by the Redskins' Mark Mosely. The crowd was so sparse, joked one player, that when they introduced the teams, the players ran up into the stands and shook hands and individually introduced themselves to the fans. The ridiculous games, which were merely an attempt by the NFLPA to prove to owners that it could field teams and play without them, would continue throughout the strike, with little success.

The strike came at a period in my life when I felt alone and very dry spiritually. Mitch, still in Chicago at seminary, had been a source of much encouragement over the phone. I decided to pay him a visit to get my mind off St. Louis. Mitch and Allison lived in an on-campus apartment, which was only a year old at the time and was pretty nice. Their furniture wasn't new. Mitch had taken a beat-up chair, purchased for five bucks at a garage sale, and tossed a sheepskin covering over the big rip that ran down the front; the long, dignified wooden legs gave it a stately appearance. Most of the living room was stacked with seminary books on tops of old chairs and K-mart shelving. But there was a new sofa bed, which had been a wedding present. That was where I collapsed and I lay talking to Mitch for several more hours.

I was in desperate need to be refreshed spiritually at the time. The pressures brought about by living in St. Louis, the strike, and all the superstar worldliness had gotten to me. I wanted to spend a few quiet days with Mitch. My first night there Mitch invited a friend, Dean Ropp, over to his place. We spent several hours studying the Word and praying. Our topic was relationships and fellowship, and how important those things were to maintaining a spiritual closeness with God. Dean started crying, and admitted how long it had been since he'd seen his brother. He told us that the relationship Mitch and I had developed was something to be proud of, and he prayed for forgiveness for not paying more attention to his family.

Mitch was still heavily involved with Young Life and headed up the local chapter at a nearby high school. Once a week they got together and played basketball. I needed to work out to keep in shape, just in case, so I accompanied Mitch to the gym the next day. We arrived early, and Mitch stood by while I hit the weight room pretty hard. The basketball coach ducked in during my workout. I pumped away on the bench press while Mitch chatted with him for a while. Finally, Mitch introduced me. "Neil Lomax," I said, shaking his hand. He smiled. "You know, there's a Neil Lomax who plays for the St. Louis Cardinals," the coach said. "People ever get you two confused?" I laughed, then realized he was serious. "Nah," I said, getting back to the weights. An hour later I was playing hoops with Mitch's Young Life crew when the coach idled into the gym. The high school kids were watching my every move, and several of them quickly explained to the coach. When it finally hit him, he turned redder than a beet. It had felt good to be anonymous.

Mitch turned out to be a spiritual oasis for me during that period of time. My problem centered around my relationship with Christ and my celebrity, and the two had somewhat merged prior to the strike. In other words, as my success went, so went my relationship with the Lord. The strike made me vividly aware of how shallow such feelings were; that my relationship with Christ had to be solid regardless of the status of my football career. I had to find a way to separate the two, and it came in the form of prayer, discussion, and Bible study with Mitch.

"Neil, remember Proverbs 16:4," Mitch said. "If a man places his hopes in God, his plans will succeed. Seek ye *first* the kingdom of God, and everything will be added unto you. You need peace, Neil, but be like the wise man and build your house on the rock."

My relationship with the Lord, up to that point, had been pretty much head knowledge, not heart knowledge. Until the strike, I really hadn't dealt with adversity. When I left Mitch, it was as if I had been given a new lease on life. I was spiritually invigorated.

When I returned to my home in St. Louis, which I shared with Keith Chancey, director of K-Life, a Christian youth ministry, I felt spiritually revived enough to help him and all his "kids." Even though Keith had asked me to get involved earlier in the strike, I had been reluctant because I had allowed my bitterness toward the union and football to affect my entire personality.

I was out riding three-wheelers with Keith when we heard the good news: The strike, after fifty-seven days, was over. That was music to my ears. We got word on Thursday, November 18, and coaches scrambled to prepare us for San Francisco in just two days. It was hard to believe. Many players had just horsed around and done absolutely nothing to stay in shape. Fortunately the game was at home, so we didn't lose any travel time. Our execution against the 49ers was pitiful. By the second quarter, everybody on the field, including the 49ers, was exhausted. Cramps were hitting everybody—a sure sign of poor conditioning. Only 38,064 fans bothered to attend, but they voiced their disapproval in throaty roars. It was a comedy of errors; I was convinced a good high school team could've beaten either club. We lost, 31–20, and I barely completed 30 percent of my passes.

Commissioner Pete Rozelle scrambled to salvage the remains of the season and settled on a nine-game season (we had already played three games), with a "Super Bowl Tournament" to follow. The normal play-off structure wouldn't be possible since enough games hadn't been played to properly eliminate teams, so the play-offs would be more wide-open.

I was looking forward to seeing more of Laurie, and the way the season had been going only encouraged my feelings. After the San Francisco loss, I wrote to her.

Laurie,

Just wanted to say hi and tell you I miss you and think about you all the time. I wanted to tell you that I'm sorry for being so gloomy lately—the strike, and then losing to San Francisco, really put me under emotionally.

Spiritually, the strike taught me a lot. I need to trust God for everything, not just football and money, but also relationships, health, emotions, everything. We need to put Him first in all that we do. I know tomorrow will come. I need to be happy and optimistic and have faith that God will take care of the rest. He says so!

Winning or losing is not the principle—it's how I handle it and what concessions I make to make myself a better human being and a better Christian. So pray for me—please! I needed to say that to you and I hope you understand. I'm glad for your support, care, and love. It means so much.

I love you, Laurie.

Neil

We eked out our next two victories over Atlanta and Philadelphia by identical scores of 23–20, and although my completion percentage rose, I really didn't perform that well. Coach Hanifan had retreated into a conservative, cautious offense, and it appeared as if we were almost scared to open it up. When things would get hairy in the late stages of a game, Hanifan would turn to Jim Hart, but Hart seldom fared any better. Hart played the last ten minutes in our 12–7 loss to Washington, then moved us close enough for Neil O'Donoghue to kick the game-winning field goal to beat Chicago, 10–7. On December 26, we faced the rising New York Giants at home. To win that game meant a spot in the play-offs, and I was determined to make it happen on my own.

By the fourth quarter, though, things looked bleak. The Giants quarterback, Scott Brunner (who is now *my* backup in St. Louis), had already completed one touchdown to my good friend John Mistler, who was having perhaps his finest game as a pro. New York then took a 21–17 lead with their second Brunner-to-Mistler touchdown in less than three minutes, and with just 1:07 on the clock, our chances for victory and an early play-off spot seemed hopeless. Just as he had done twice before, Hanifan turned to Hart. I was livid, then shocked, when Hart said no. "My arm's too cold," he told Hanifan. I wondered if he was thinking more along the lines that he was tired of bailing me out and was eager to see me fail. Quickly I snapped my helmet back on; I determined to rise to the challenge. Dave Ahrens returned a squib kickoff to our 30-yard line, and I realized I was facing 70 yards of bad road with just sixty seconds to do it. Like my miracle days at Portland State, a soothing calm enveloped me. On first down, I hit Roy Green on an out pattern for 26 yards, then threaded a 36-yard needle to Willard Harrell. Finally, with only twenty seconds left and running for my life I found Roy open in the end zone for a game-winning, 8-yard touchdown.

The same crowd that had booed when I came on the field a minute earlier went berserk, exploding into bedlam. Afterwards, reporters crushed around my locker so tightly I could hardly move. "I didn't feel any pressure," I answered Dennis Dillon, a *Globe-Democrat* sportswriter, matter-of-factly. "I wasn't nervous at all. I kind of surprised myself; God filled me with His love, and I felt a really good rush of confidence. I just thought that whatever happened was meant to happen."

The Giants game was a day of growth for me. The two weeks prior to that game had been tough; I'd been hassled by the press and by fans. But I had put more pressure on myself than anyone else. I was learning more and more to stay in the pocket when the rush was on, to be patient and allow pass patterns to develop. I still needed to improve a little more in third-and-long situations, but my performance against the Giants had hushed most doubters.

Super Bowl-bound Washington blanked us, 28–0, in our last regular-season game, but we limped into the play-offs nonetheless. We wound up playing Green Bay in temperatures that would make a bear shiver. Mitch had a friend who was a pilot, and they and two other friends flew down in a private plane for the game. I couldn't believe the crowd. It seemed like everybody was in bright orange or green hunting gear, drunk as a skunk, obnoxious, and throwing snowballs everywhere. We started out strong, marching more than 70 yards for a touchdown. My confidence was high, my passes crisp, and O. J. Anderson was making big bursts up the middle. But the Packers were just hot, and quarterback Lynn Dickey put on an aerial show. I matched him bullet for bullet, but we just couldn't get the ball in the end zone when it counted. We lost, 31–16, despite my 365 yards passing—the most ever by an NFL quarterback in his first play-off game. The season hadn't been a total loss; our young team had proved it could win in the face of adversity. I wondered how good we might have been without the strike.

The strike didn't accomplish anything for the union that couldn't have been accomplished through more reasonable means. Players did make gains but NFL club owners lost between $182 and $217 million because of the strike, while the players lost $63 million overall in salaries.

The union felt that salary inequities had been somewhat corrected through the wage scale, and that some measure of protection was provided to older veterans through the severance pay article. The main issue, percentage of the gross or percentage of TV revenue, was not achieved, but postseason pay was doubled. To me, it was sort of a standoff, with both sides claiming certain victories. The strike was bloody war, and both sides gave in on issues that had led to it, making it, in my opinion, a giant waste of time, talent, games, and paychecks.

*   *   *

Back home in Portland that winter, Laurie and I continued to get closer to each other. The more I was around her the more I wanted to be around her, but I still played a cat-and-mouse game occasionally. It's my belief that a guy shouldn't just throw himself at a girl and immediately begin pouring out his heart and thoughts to her. I've always been cautious in relationships, just kind of checking out the other person. I thought keeping Laurie guessing about what my true feelings were, would keep up her interest. But I was fascinated by her, as well as by her family. Her parents are truly special people. Her father, Jerry Exley, is a successful banker, but he never mentions his career. He had been a standout football, basketball, and baseball player in high school, and had even played some minor league baseball in the Brooklyn Dodgers organization. The Dodgers were my team, so I *had* to like him for that. A handsome guy, Jerry is just a shade over six feet tall, trim and darkly tanned, with curly gray hair. Jerry and I hit it off right away, and we became regular tennis opponents. He's very good at tennis, and I rarely beat him. We're both very competitive and often the intensity of our games would make you think you were at a real tournament.

Laurie's mother, Donna, is a cultured, pretty schoolteacher, with an unmatchable personality. It's easy to see where Laurie gets the sparkle in her eyes, as well as her easygoing style. Mrs. Exley is a great conversationalist, and is very conscientious about whatever task she has at hand. She sings in the church choir, is a tremendous tennis player, and all-American mom. Laurie's parents have a special marriage. Though both have different interests, the first thing I noticed was that they are always quick to compromise. Their rapport is simple, gentle, and loving. They deal with problems straightforwardly, then move on. I liked their example.

Little did I know that Laurie was telling her mother every detail about our relationship—a fact I would later come to appreciate. Laurie thinks so much of her mother as a friend that she shared every twist and turn of our relationship with her. Her mother's advice, thank God, was usually perfect and always reaffirmed the importance of turning to God with every problem.

My old friend, Stu Gaussoin was also on hand that summer. He had really suffered when his football career came to an end, though he was still refusing to accept that. His senior season had been unspectacular, and his knee had not healed properly. A shot at the pros in Canada also turned out to be a dead-end for Stu. But his way of ignoring his problems seemed to be to just party. He had several job offers, but he couldn't seem to stick with anything. Though we hadn't seen a lot of each other, we spoke over the phone pretty frequently.

For some reason, that off-season we began hitting it off again. The old feelings we'd had through high school and college started coming back. Robin Pflugrad, my college buddy, was coaching receivers at PSU now, and he had moved into my house with me. Stu began hinting how nice it could be if he moved in, too. "It'll be just like old times," he kept saying. Telling him "nah," each time, I held him at bay, but Stu could sense I was weakening with each request. I still cared a lot about Stu, but my success sometimes made me feel awkward.

Stu had no qualms about spending my money when we were out together. At the time, it didn't bother me, but I didn't think it would be a good idea to have him living with us. As it was, he was staying over three or four nights a week. And he always needed money for gas or something.

Stu was never at a loss for words. He knew my feelings about his life-style, and he was aware that that was one way to get to me. He was constantly telling me, "I've really been trying spiritually, Neil," he'd say. "I'm going to church a lot." I couldn't help but remember how we'd found Christ together at Camp Malibu. For Stu's sake, I hoped he was telling me the truth.

Just before I left for my third season in St. Louis, Stu came to me in a rare emotional state. We had had a tremendous time during the off-season, but I had made no mention of allowing him to move in with Robin and me. With his voice breaking, Stu told me he had been seeking spiritual counsel. "I need a place to live, Neil," he said. "I want to straighten my life out. I'm making a serious effort this time with God. Please just let me live at your place while I work things out." I sensed a sincere change, so, against my better judgment, I consented.

The off-season had been a pretty inconclusive one, although my relationship with Laurie had been a bright exception. My brother Terry married Rebecca Lee Brattain on June 17, 1983, and then launched himself into a career as a youth adviser at Mountain Park Church. If I was grateful for anything, it was that both my brothers were intense in their relationships with Christ.

When I arrived at camp, I was introduced to Paul Dowhower, the newly hired offensive coordinator and quarterback coach who had been lured away from the Denver Broncos. From the firm grip of his handshake to his steely blue eyes, I sensed he was all business, the kind of coach I needed to push me. He had a long history of providing just the punch teams needed in their offenses.

He had coached quarterbacks and receivers for the St. Louis Cardinals under Don Coryell in 1973. During that season, Jim Hart had completed a club record 55.6 percent of his passes, and five Cardinal receivers caught at least twenty-nine passes. He moved on to UCLA as offensive coordinator under Dick Vermeil, and the Bruins won the 1976 Rose Bowl behind his explosive offense. He emerged two years later as the quarterback coach at Stanford and was promoted to head coach in 1979. During his tenure at Stanford, Rod had helped groom future NFL players James Lofton, Steve Dils, Turk Schonert, and Darrin Nelson.

Clearly an innovative offensive mind, Rod was well-schooled in the passing game. A strict technician, he told me his intentions were to overhaul my form and style, piece by piece. Imperfections in my motion would be remedied or eliminated. "You don't have to be the hero," he said. "Just do your job exactly right. When you are totally sure and confident in what you're doing, everything else will fall into place."

Rod took me back to school. Never had I been pushed harder or longer. He totally streamlined and refined my style. He went over and over my dropback, watching with skeptical, critical eyes, looking for one mistake, one error in my form. My footwork, he said, was crucial; so he taught me precisely how to stand, how to push off when throwing, how to get more velocity on the football. We watched game films until my bloodshot eyes ached, as Rod painstakingly showed me how to make quicker defensive reads, how to recognize coverages just a little faster. As camp wore on, I was learning fast and getting more comfortable with every snap.

My learning was interrupted the week before our first preseason game, when we traveled to London to play the Minnesota Vikings in the first American football game ever played on English soil. We had all guessed the trip would be "quite a bother," and we were right. England's probably a great place to go on a vacation, but when you add in all the headaches of trying to play a professional football game in a totally different environment, it becomes a real nuisance. The eight-hour flight across the Atlantic wasn't a joyride, either. Nevertheless, I was pretty excited about seeing London.

Bringing America's favorite sport to London's Wembley Stadium had presented countless problems. Goalposts were built at a cost of $6,000. Cheerleaders were recruited from a United States Air Force base outside London. Both teams were forced to shower and dress at the hotel; Wembley Stadium, which seats eighty thousand, has neither locker rooms nor showers. The British people had no idea what the game was about. A hand-lettered poster outside a souvenir stand offered fans the *Illustrated NFL Playbook*, calling it "your pro football guide—blitzes, bombs, etc. explained."

While getting there was a royal pain, the game was fun. More than a preseason game, it was an event. It was like opening your season to all the fanfare usually given a Super Bowl. The Fleet Band of the Royal Marines played "The Star-Spangled Banner" and "God Save the Queen," as the 32,847 befuddled fans roared like an American crowd 100,000 strong. The fans never really understood what we were doing, but screamed in adulation at every long run, long pass, or spectacular hit. We lost, 28–10, but the experience was enlightening.

The account of the game as reported by the English press was also fascinating. "The missing ingredient was partisan support, the feeling of identification and involvement," wrote Clem Thomas in the *Observer*. "Instead, the crowd was educating itself into another American attack on their culture, and trying to decide if they enjoyed the flavour. It was the same with Kentucky Fried Chicken and McDonald's burgers."

Alan Hoby of the *Express* didn't seem pleased with the exhibition. "All those endless collisions of outsized flesh and blood . . . all those baffling hand signals and free coded rhythmic grunts which only players of their own side could understand . . . and all those coaches barking orders . . . to an outsider, it was a disorganized mess. A big bore."

For one thing, the trip certainly put the game into perspective for me, and it was interesting to see how others view the sport without having been surrounded by it all their lives. I chuckled at how primitive and disorganized the sport must have appeared.

The trip was exhausting. We spent only seventy-two hours in London, which gave the whole club a giant case of double jet lag at a most crucial time during preseason. But the coaches had set us on a killer pace, and we kept our spirits high. We beat the Bears the next week in overtime, 27–24, and Rod told me I had played a fine game, but was quick to point out my remaining weaknesses. Nothing got past "Rocket" Rod; he had pinpointed my every fault.

The week after the Bears game, Hanifan approached me as we worked out in the summer heat of training camp. "I watched the films of the Bears game," he said, reaching for a cigarette. "I saw a lot of refinement on your part. Everything about you looks better. Your drops, your footwork, setting up—all those factors. When I saw the film, I thought, *Holy catfish! Neil's arrived!*" I grinned modestly as Hanifan patted my helmet and walked on.

*   *   *

A separated shoulder on opening day forced me to miss the first three games of the season. We dropped all three games. I was learning our new offense, but things were falling into place a piece at a time. I could sense it was only a matter of time before everything would mesh. After one particularly grueling practice session at Busch Stadium, I took my shower and started the long walk from the locker rooms to the parking lot. The Cardinals offices are located in the basement of the stadium, and when we exit the locker room, we come out into the offices, down a long hall, and through the front of the building where all the secretaries and executive offices are located.

My hair was still wet, as I grabbed my black Nike gym bag and loped down the hall. My legs ached from the day-to-day pounding on the Astroturf, although my unlaced Air Jordan sneakers helped ease the pain of my blistered feet. When I neared the door, one of the secretaries glanced up. "You have a visitor," she smiled, tapping her pencil on the desk and nodding her head toward the waiting room. Two other girls giggled. I looked at them blankly, unaware of the source of their humor.

When I opened the door to the lobby, I couldn't believe my eyes. A girl with long, bleached blond hair sat waiting. Her makeup was applied with a technician's skill, as heavy black mascara and deep blue eyeshadow flattered her piercing blue eyes. Bright red lipstick brought attention to her shiny, heart-shaped mouth. Tight, black leather pants left not a single curve or muscle movement to the imagination. Her left leg was crossed in alluring fashion over her right, the tight leather tracing her streamlined legs all the way down to her high-heeled red shoes. A leather top plunged way below modesty at her chest. I blushed, realizing I was staring. "Neil," she asked, pulling her soft-looking hair away from her face. "Can we talk for a minute?" She stood up. I was still speechless. I could feel the eyes of every secretary in the office piercing my back. I had never seen this woman before in my life; a fact the secretaries would never believe.

"Let's talk outside," I said, moving toward the door with embarrassment. I could swear I heard giggles from inside the office. They had seen football groupies before. We stepped outside. "I met a teammate of yours last night," she said. "He's out with my girl friend. We're from out of town. Well, he said you'd probably be glad to go out with me, and to wait for you at the end of practice." I shook my head. "He was mistaken. I have a date tonight, but thanks for the thought."

"But they left me here without a ride," she insisted, her confidence shaken. She moved up next to me. "It's only 3:00 P.M. Can't you just take me to meet them?"

Reluctantly, I gave in. As we walked to my car, I felt like every person in St. Louis was watching me. Admittedly, I was having trouble not looking at this girl. Half of me was saying "be careful," the other half was urging me to do what came naturally. This sort of temptation is always there for an athlete. Just as there are men who are attracted by money, there are women who are attracted by celebrity.

The St. Louis freeway was already busy as we headed across town to the bar where this girl's friend and my teammate were supposed to be. The entire ride my visitor just leaned up against the door of the car and looked at me, talking in a breathy whisper. I realized I was sweating; I rolled down my window, allowing a blast of cool, autumn St. Louis air to fill the car. We talked about the weather, the economy, politics, and football—anything I could think of to take my mind off her and the reason she was there. It was comical, really. I avoided anything personal. We finally reached the bar where her friends were supposed to be, but they weren't there. "Don't leave me here," she said. "What if they don't come back?"

The situation was getting ridiculous. "Why don't we go to your place and you can call your friend from there?" she said. We turned around and zoomed back out on the freeway. I knew going to my place would be flirting with trouble. When we pulled into the parking lot of my building my heart fell to my knees. Sitting there waiting was the girl with whom I had a date. I never slowed down, hoping she hadn't seen me. We zipped right back out of the parking lot. "Where are we going?" the girl asked.

"Uh, I forgot that I need to buy a shower curtain," I answered, snatching at the first thing that came to my mind. I had wanted to pick up a shower curtain on my way home that day. We whipped into a nearby K mart. I jumped out. "Uh, why don't you just wait here," I said. "I'll only be a minute." For the next thirty minutes I paced back and forth in front of the shower curtain display, wondering why one of my teammates would do this to me, wondering where I should drop her off, and wondering how I had gotten myself into this predicament, and laughing woefully at myself. I guess I wasn't looking too cool—but I was trying to be honest, and it wasn't easy. It's still not easy. I finally made my purchase and went back out to the car, hoping she would be gone. No way. There was only one way out of the problem. "Look," I said. "I have to get home." She looked at me longingly, and I turned my eyes away. Without saying another word, I drove her back to the prearranged meeting place, feeling rather silly. We arrived back at the lounge, and she swung her long legs around and stepped from the car.

"Bye," she said. I waved out the window, then zoomed home. In all the excitement, I'd forgotten that Mitch and Allison were coming in to stay a few days. They were due at 6:00 P.M.; it was five minutes till. I whipped into the parking lot. My date's car was empty. Perhaps she'd gone to wait at my door, I thought. My mind raced; I prayed she hadn't seen me. I found her outside and nervously explained that practice had taken a little longer than normal. We rushed into my condo, and I fell into a chair with a sigh. Simultaneously, the doorbell rang, and Mitch and Allison walked inside.

"You look like you've had a pretty boring afternoon," Mitch said, giving me a solid hug.

"If you only knew, man," I said.

Tuesday, November 15, 1983. The ringing telephone interrupted my preparations for Sunday's upcoming game against the San Diego Chargers. I dropped my playbook and picked up the receiver.

"Mr. Lomax?" inquired a firm male voice. "This is your insurance company in Portland. We have a report that your BMW has been wrecked, but you told us it would be in storage while you were playing in St. Louis. We can't have you coming back to Portland and driving your car without telling us, because you're not insured."

I hadn't been back to Portland. Telling the agent I'd get back with him, I hung up the phone. Stu! I called Robin and got the story. Unbeknownst to me, Stu had been telling Robin that I'd given him permision to host parties, drive my BMW, and make long-distance phone calls. Robin minded his own business, and Stu took advantage of it.

After the insurance agent called, I started thinking. My parents had warned me weeks earlier that they had spotted Stuart driving my car. Not once, but several times. I had called him directly, and feigning innocence, Stu told me my family was mistaken. "I haven't been driving your car, except maybe once or twice. Everything's fine," he had said. The whole thing had become an unnecessary distraction. I could've kicked myself for ever letting him move in. When the phone call came from the insurance company, that cinched it.

It wasn't the car; it wasn't the money; it wasn't the unpaid bills. The lies hurt more than anything. When you can't trust a friend anymore, the entire relationship has no basis whatsoever. I picked up the phone and called Robin, and we talked for a long time about the situation.

I was shocked. I wanted to believe differently, but the facts were on the table.

My attitude changed from surprise to anger. Over the next few weeks Robin and I did some checking, and we found out that within a matter of months, my credit rating, my house, and my car were a mess. Stu had not only wrecked my car, but he had it repaired at a cheap fix-it place to hide the accident.

I prayed long and hard about what action I should take. What was right, how far did loyalty go, what about old times, what was right for Stu? There was a lot involved. Stu and I had grown up together; we were going to be pals for life.

"Neil, you know that Proverbs 19:5 says that a guy has got to tell the truth or take the consequences," Robin told me.

I had to agree. It was clear that Stu had to go.

All the personal distractions were taking their toll on my performance on the field; I was having problems concentrating. After our horrible 2–6 start we battled back into contention and showed spurts of brilliance. When we rolled into Dallas for a Thanksgiving clash, we had struggled to a 5–7–1 record. Early in the game I hooked up with Roy Green for a 71-yard touchdown, but that was the only thing we did right that afternoon. Dallas bombed us, 35–17, which made the four-day weekend a very long one.

We finished the year 8–7–1, but we were notably improved by season's end. In our last two games we upset the mighty Los Angeles Raiders, 34–24, and Philadelphia, 31–7, and Rod Dowhower was already excited about the next season. "All this club needs is maturity," he said. "We're right on track."

I was eager to get home and get my personal problems ironed out. The entire flight back I wrestled with how I should handle Stu. I could still see him suffering on the trainer's table after his knee injury. I wondered what his life might've been like if he hadn't been hurt. It was going to be a painful ordeal, but my wrecked BMW and the money it had taken me to get my house and bills back in order offered me the motivation to get it over with.

When we sat down, Stu immediately tried to explain. "Let's talk about this," he pleaded. I waved him off. "Stu, this is for your own good," I told him. "You have to move." I begged him to remember the life-changing decision we had made together years before. At one time our relationship served to hold us accountable, but now, it was a case of who could get away with what. "Stu, you've lost sight of God. You've got to straighten yourself out, man. I can't help you do that. In fact, I may be contributing to the problem. You gotta go!"

Just when I thought things couldn't get any worse, I went to visit my folks. When I stepped into their house, I couldn't believe my eyes; everywhere I looked there were pictures of me. Clip-pings—with bold, color photos—stared back at me from gold frames. Trophies gleamed from every corner of the room. The normally drab walls seemed to scream Cardinal red from ceiling to floor. At least eight photo albums with news clippings dating back to high school were all over the place. I was flabbergasted. My mother met me at the door and embraced me. "Neil," she said, pecking my cheek. "Come in and tell us about the season."

The season. Who cares about the season? I was back in Port-land to *forget* the season. Then I noticed Mom was wearing a red sweater with a white Cardinal helmet stitched over the left breast. Dad peered over his glasses from across the room. "Saw your game against the Raiders on TV last week," he said. "I told the guys at work you deserve to make the play-offs, especially after the way you played. I hated to see your season end, son."

That was it. The more I looked around the house, the more upset I became. Since my college days at Portland State, there had been a slow transformation. Gone were the pictures of Valorie playing high school basketball. Gone were the school pictures of Mitch and Terry. Gone were the paintings Terry had painstakingly done for Mom and Dad. Everything was focused on me. Cardinals stickers, magnets, key chains everywhere. Action photos, sideline photos, stand-up photos. Clippings, awards, plaques. The house had become a shrine to Neil Lomax.

One of my traits is brutal honesty, which isn't always good. Sometimes I really hurt others' feelings because I just say what's in my heart, no matter how tough. I knew I had reached the point where I had to tell my parents how I felt. In my not-so-nice way, I beckoned my parents to the sofa.

"Mom, Dad, I've had it," I said. My mother shot me a puzzled look. "I am not worthy of my own shrine. I am your son. Nothing more. I am your son, who happens to play a stupid game for a living. But I've become something you brag about. You wear your Cardinals sweaters and jackets and shirts so everybody knows who you are. I don't mind you wearing that stuff, but not all the time."

My voice was choking, and the words were getting tougher. It hurt to talk to my parents like this. My dad was looking rather bewildered; my mother was clearly wounded by my remarks.

"I'm sorry," I said. "But have you stopped to think how I feel about this whole situation? All the time I'm in St. Louis, people like me because of who I am. They want my autograph or a sweatband or a chin strap. They want to talk football. When I come home, I want to be home. I want to be *Neil*. I don't want to be the Cardinals' quarterback twelve months a year."

Tears were welling in Mom's eyes, which made it tougher to go on. Dad leaned back, crossed his arms, and sighed.

"Please," I asked. "Please just be my parents. Don't be fans." My mother sniffed. "That's hard to do," she said. "We're proud of you."

"That's fine, Mom. But put it in perspective. Look at this house," I paused, pointing at the walls and bookshelves that were adorned with me. "Whatever happened to your other three children? Are you not proud of them anymore? Are they any less your children because they're not pro athletes?"

"Well maybe if you would talk to us more, it would be different," Dad interjected. "We never hear from you. You never call, you never write, you virtually ignore us."

"I know, Dad," I replied. "And I'm wrong. But think of all the people who are demanding my time now. That doesn't make you guys any less important, though. I'm at fault, too."

"Son, the trophies and the pictures and the sweaters and everything is just our way of associating ourselves with you," Dad said softly. "We miss you. We love you. We want to feel a part of your life. This is our way of trying to fit in."

I felt a little guilty. I had made my point. And I had learned something too.

"I will try to do better," I said. "But this stuff"—I pointed around the room—"has to come down. I can't come back to this. I hope you understand that if I didn't love you and Mitch, Val, and Terry I wouldn't care."

Those ordeals capped the toughest personal year in my life. Kicking my best friend out of my house, as well as telling my parents how I felt about their reaction to my stardom, were hard, but important, decisions.

When I visited my parents a few days later at Christmas, there was no evidence of their "famous" son. Pictures of Val, Mitch, and Terry had made conspicuous returns atop the television set and on various bookshelves. My "sermon on the couch," as Mitch coined it, had been effective.

The family seemed to draw closer that Christmas; there was the feeling that we were all growing together. My personal thoughts centered around Laurie and what the future held. My maturity as a pro quarterback was right on schedule, and I felt great things were looming on the horizon.

In January I got word that Jim Hart had been released. That proved how much confidence Rod Dowhower had in my abilities.

The media swarmed me for my reaction, which was simple but blunt. "Out with the old, in with the new," I said. "I just hope when it's my time to go, I won't hang around too long. I would want to give a young guy a chance." Inside I was totally relieved that management had decided to put a stop to the friction on the sidelines between me and Jim Hart. It would be a load off my mind as I entered my third season.

In the meantime, I had been working out religiously with Dieter Zander, director of music at our church. Putting in more time in the weight room than ever before, I busted my butt in preparation for the season. Dieter and I made a little pact: He would lift with me three times a week, and I would study the Bible with him throughout the week. I grew not only physically, but also spiritually, as my fourth season approached.

10

The Year of Living Famously

"Neil hates to lose. It can be basketball, softball, or checkers. He'd be happy to give back 90 percent of his salary if he could win the Super Bowl. Winning is very, very important to him. If he says different, he's lying."

—Mitch Lomax

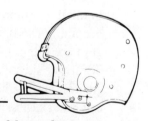

Disguising my feelings for Laurie, which I had been doing remarkably well, was getting much harder as we entered 1984. We had been dating a great deal and it was becoming apparent she was the one for me. But I didn't want to sell God short, I wanted to be sure I was moving in His will. Meanwhile, my playing coy had terribly frustrated Laurie, who later told me she had sensed from the start that I was the only one she could spend the rest of her life with. Because of my cat-and-mouse game, she was growing terribly impatient, wondering how three years of dating could pass by without some indication of how I felt about our future.

Spring came and nothing had changed. We were spending virtually every day together, but I refused to allow Laurie to peek inside my heart and see my true feelings. Tired and confused, she had told her mother that she was emotionally drained and had had enough of my games, and was on the verge of telling me to forget it, because she felt I might never be able to make a commitment. I, too, was struggling with my emotions, but for different reasons. I had no doubts; I just wanted to be absolutely positive about my decision. In May I went to St. Louis for mini-camp and returned with an engagement ring. Trusting the Lord to guide me, I basically said, "God, I got the ring, so You show me now if she's not the one. And quick!" I had made up my mind, oblivious to the fact that while I was giving in to my heart and drawing closer to her, she was feeling more and more unsure of me.

I picked July 4, 1984, as my deadline to propose to her, which gave me two more months to think it over. At the beginning of those two months, I was thinking about whether or not Laurie was the right one; but the more I prayed, the more God revealed to me it was more a matter of working on myself, my attitude, on becoming the right one for her. It occurred to me that so many guys are hung up on choosing the right girl, like she's got to be beautiful, she's got to have a great figure, she's got to have the greatest smile, she's got to have this or that. Guys think if they can find all these things, they'll love their wife more. For me, that wasn't the case at all. God began teaching *me* to be more self-less, to be more of a servant, to learn to honor this girl I was going to marry. Love is more than emotions; it's something you nurture. Through prayer, I matured a great deal during those two months.

The weekend before the Fourth of July, Laurie was trying to talk to me about her future, about saving money, about finding a place to live, and about "how hard these questions are for a single girl to answer." I just smiled and said, "You never know." Unbeknownst to me, that had been an attempt to entice the truth from my lips, to test my reactions toward a potential engagement. Her effort netted nothing, and she was crushed, convinced that I would leave her in limbo in a few weeks to head for another training camp. She told her mother that she refused to go another season without some sort of commitment and made up her mind to tell me she would be dating other people. Her deadline for the bad news: the Fourth of July.

The next week, as Laurie plotted what would be a painful escape from our relationship, I plotted how I would present her with the ring. Neither of us was aware of the other's intentions. I was full of ideas on how to surprise her with the diamond. Maybe take her for Chinese food and have the ring delivered in a fortune cookie. Nah, too difficult. Maybe take her fishing, tie it to her line, and then she'd reel it in. Nah, much too risky. I decided I'd keep it simple.

Laurie's family owns a cabin in Washington State, just across the Columbia River, located on Wauna Lake, a serene body of water surrounded by sky-reaching fir trees, white-capped mountains, and peaceful woods. That's where she and I went on the Fourth of July with most of our families. That night we sat out on the back porch, watching the setting sun burn the edges of the high-topped trees with a deep, subtle orange. The fading light blinked off the rippling lake with the glimmer of a new coin; the lap, lap, lap of the water against the dock was soothing. Crickets were chirping all around, and darkness was already setting in throughout the deep woods. *This is perfect,* I thought.

"Hey, Laurie," I said. "Let's go for a boat ride." The stillness was broken only by the putter of the six-horsepower motor on the back of our tiny fishing boat as we headed quietly toward the heart of Wauna Lake.

I killed the engine. The atmosphere was tense, and I decided to seek God's help as I pondered the toughest question of my life. I asked Laurie to lead us in a few words of prayer. She really didn't want to, but I insisted. "It would mean a lot to me if you would,"

I told her. She had no idea why, but she finally obliged. Laurie's prayer asked for God's guidance in our lives, as well as in my upcoming season. Meanwhile, I quietly slipped the ring box from the pocket of my jacket. I closed the prayer myself. "Oh, God, I know this is Your will." I opened my eyes, looked straight at Laurie, and dropped to one knee. "Laurie, will you marry me?"

She was surprised. Her eyes brimmed with tears and she gave me the fiercest hug of my life. "Yes, Neil, yes." We were both so excited we were speechless; I would have been more so had I known how close I'd come to losing her. As we embraced, there was no doubt Laurie was the person I wanted to spend the rest of my life with.

Laurie's folks gave us a big engagement party the next week at the lake. Both my family and Laurie's family got together with a lot of our friends, and we had a great time. Balloons and crepe paper were everywhere, and rowboat races and grilled hamburgers were the order of the afternoon, a sample of celebrations that were yet to come. On the way home Laurie and I set the wedding date for February 9, 1985.

By the time I readied to fly to St. Louis, the upcoming season seemed a bit anticlimatic. Turning my attention from Laurie to football wasn't exactly an easy affair.

Training camp had been underway a very short time when my agent, Leigh Steinberg, got right down to basics with the Cardinals on my new contract demands. The 1984 season would be the final year of my contract, and the Cardinals desperately wanted my name on a new pact. Mouse had started coaching in the United States Football League and was making a lot of racket about signing me when I became a free agent at the end of the season, which frightened the Cardinals. Furthermore, the team had pruned Joe Sullivan from the front-office tree, and Leigh was dealing with the team's new negotiator, Bob Wallace, a more open, easygoing guy. Compared with those in my rookie season, negotiations were a snap. On July 25, the Cardinals made me the highest-paid player in team history with a four-year contract, which was "guaranteed, regardless of skill or injury." That kind of guarantee had been our primary goal. Overnight, I'd shot up to among the top ten quarterback salaries in the NFL. I couldn't believe it—what a raise!

Rod Dowhower's extra effort the year before was producing long-awaited results as the Cardinals entered their "Silver Anniversary" twenty-fifth season. The entire offensive unit was displaying a confidence we'd never felt before, and Rod's scheme worked to perfection in the preseason. Basically, we used the same package used by the San Diego Chargers, who were coached by Don Coryell, Rod's former boss. Rod utilized the backs not only as runners, but as receivers in screens and flare control routes. He also emphasized down-the-field passing to the wide receivers and tight ends. Not only were we opening it up more, but the team was beginning to *believe* we were capable of controlling the line of scrimmage. It felt more like my college days.

Rod's meticulous work habits and precise demands prompted me to refer to him as "Professor," and he continued working on my timing and delivery. "Neil, you're the focal point of not just the offense, but the whole team," he said. "It's not fair to ask you to be a hero every week; just go out and be proficient and efficient." Proficient and efficient. "You're the type player who can give us the winning edge," he kept insisting through training camp. "That's all we can ask from you."

I believed him. Coach Hanifan, too, could sense we were on the brink of something big, and he spared no words in expressing the importance of the season. "We want to win," he yelled one afternoon, as sixty-some helmeted players stood sweat-soaked in the hundred-degree temperatures of training camp.

"I don't give a rat's rear end how, we just have to win. I was mad last year. We didn't play worth a nickel at the beginning of the season. We went 1–5, then finished 8–7–1. If we had played well to start with, we'd have been in the play-offs." He was pacing now, puffing deeply on his Vantages. "That's why it's so critical for us to get off to a fast start. If we do that, we've got the personnel within this team now that we'll be tough down the stretch." With mimicked enthusiasm, we whooped and hollered like high school kids on the first day of varsity practice. Like a cheerleader at a pep rally, Hanifan spent much of his time convincing us of our potential and injecting us with optimism. "We will have a helluva team," he predicted. "A helluva team."

We opened at Green Bay, and the offense looked great, and I felt especially good. But our defense and the special teams killed us. Kicker Neil O'Donoghue missed an extra point that might have resulted in an overtime period, and he missed a 45-yard field goal try that might have won the game with 2:15 to play. A kickoff was returned 54 yards by the Packers' Harlan Huckleby to set up another score. We lost, 24–23. We won easily against the Bills, then took victory from the Colts when I threw fourth-quarter touchdowns of 47 and 56 yards to Roy Green for a 34–33 win.

We lost a heartbreaker at New Orleans and came home to face Dan Marino and the Miami Dolphins; Dan and I squared off like gunfighters at the OK Corral. We lost, 36–28, but 46,991 fans were given a treat. "I've been around long enough to witness quite a few shoot-outs, but this one was among the best," Dolphins head coach Don Shula remarked after Marino threw for 429 yards and I passed for 308. We weren't winning like we'd hoped, but the Cards had historically been a late-starting team. For certain, we could move the ball and score.

We were five weeks into the season before we really realized how good we could be. Against the Dallas Cowboys, no less, our division nemesis. Going into the game, with two wins and three losses, I realized we were in a must-win situation; we had already let several games get away.

Against the vaunted Dallas blitz, however, we exploded. I completed nineteen of twenty-nine passes, almost all in the face of the blitz, for 354 yards and three touchdowns. Roy Green had his best day as a receiver in the NFL, catching eight passes for 189 yards and two touchdowns. We knew we could be contenders, and now we were showing it on the field. With approximately 80 percent of the CBS-TV viewing audience watching the game, it was a great opportunity to prove to the entire nation we could play.

The first big play came on a third and nine at our 30-yard line. The Cowboys' blitz poured in from everywhere, but Roy cut across the middle, I saw him a split second before I was hit, and I fired. Roy made the catch in full stride, broke a tackle by Victor Scott, and outran everybody else for a 70-yard touchdown. Minutes later, after we recovered a Tony Dorsett fumble, I called a simple square-out play to Roy, designed to get a first down. When I approached the line of scrimmage, however, I sensed Dallas would blitz again, so I audibled off at the line when I noticed their tight man-to-man coverage. "Check, White, 989, . . . White. 989 . . . hut . . . hutt!" Roy streaked down the right sideline, beating Cowboys cornerback Everson Walls by a step, and I hit him with a perfect over-the-shoulder spiral for a 45-yard touchdown and a 31–13 lead.

Roy came back to the sideline panting with excitement. I hugged him. "We have the offense! We can do it!" he said, showing a new sense of respect. "Those guys are giving us chances for big plays." Randy White, the Cowboys' superstar defensive line—Randy White, "Too Tall" Jones, and Harvey Martin—didn't get near me all day, thanks to superb play by guards Terry Stieve and Joe Bostic, tackles Luis Sharpe and Tootie Robbins, and my center Randy Clark. The final count was 31–20, and we were filled with confidence: It was the first time in six years the Cardinals had beaten the Cowboys in Dallas.

The next week's game against the formidable Chicago Bears was one of the most punishing I'd ever seen. Linebackers Mike Singletary and Todd Bell were everywhere, and their collisions with our running backs and receivers sounded like trees falling. But big plays from our defense kept us in great field position, which made it a pretty easy day for the offense. Chicago's starting cornerback, rookie Shaun Gayle from Ohio State, became my favorite target on the afternoon, as Roy turned 'im and burned 'im time after time. When I saw Gayle line up on Roy man-to-man, just 3 or 4 yards off the line. I almost laughed out loud. Carl Lewis can't stay with Roy Green when he's healthy, much less a confused rookie. On the fourth play of the game, we isolated Roy on the youngster, and with the quickness of a snake I hit him on a 54-yard touchdown right over the middle, into the heart of the Bears' defense. "We've got it, babe," I told him afterward. The attitude on the sideline was entirely different from years past. Late in the fourth quarter I scrambled 9 yards for another touchdown and elatedly spiked the ball into the turf. "That looked like a white man's spike," Roy laughed. The racial problems on this team were long gone. We won, 38–21, against the team that would eventually come within one game of the Super Bowl.

In the midst of all the fun, we were unaware of just how well the team was doing. We were leading the National Football Conference with 416.1 yards per game, and in just six weeks I'd thrown for 2,007 yards and 12 touchdowns. Our average of 30.7 points a game was tops in the NFC, and Roy Green's 21.4 yards per catch was best in the NFL. "Statistics are fine," Rod Dowhower kept saying in practice. "But they don't mean anything if you don't win."

We owed a lot of those stats to Rod, who had quit calling the boring, conservative plays that were commonplace during my first couple seasons. Rod continued to work hard with me, taking me on the field every week and breaking down every play into a "progression" procedure. It meant learning where to progress if my primary receiver was covered, then where to progress if my secondary receiver was covered. It was a painstaking task; the system required snap judgment through knowledge of the offense.

There was no room for errors. His pet peeve was my impatience in waiting for pass routes to develop. "When I tell you to drop seven steps and nine yards deep, it's to let the pass patterns develop," he instructed. "Sometimes you see things developing and cut off your drop around five yards. Then, your receivers aren't fully into their patterns, the defense is in your face, and your blockers have no idea where you are. Obviously, the play isn't going to work when you do that." Rod was stubborn, but he was molding me into a first-rate NFL quarterback.

Jim Hart had signed with the Washington Redskins, and the eighth week of the season he came to town with his new team— as the backup to Joe Theismann. I really didn't have much to say. Comments were being passed from St. Louis to Washington, but I was toning down my remarks in the hopes of letting the Jim Hart situation die. I was having the year of my life with the Cardinals, and I refused to let an old skeleton come rattling out of the closet. Ironically, if I threw a touchdown pass against the Redskins, I would set the club record for most consecutive games with at least one—I was tied with Charlie Johnson for the lead with 16.

Everything in my life seemed to be going right, and the Lord had brought me a long way from the strike-delayed season in 1982. When you've been through some tough times, the good times are so much sweeter. But after tasting the bitter waters of failure, I was careful not to get swept away in the wave of publicity the team was riding on. Admittedly, it was exciting; we were winning, I was engaged, I had a new contract, and I was developing enriching friendships with most of my new teammates. Roy Green and I had become close buddies, and were constantly together. He's married and has two beautiful little girls, and his wife cooks great meals that look and taste like they're right out of Good Housekeeping. "You want me to keep throwing the ball to your husband," I told her one evening while stuffing myself, "you just keep having me over for these meals." O. J. Anderson lived only a block away, and we'd often study for Sunday's game together, eat chicken wings, and play cards. We were all friends, not just teammates.

Yet, for all the tranquility and excitement the season was bringing, I couldn't rid my thoughts of Laurie. Being around Pat Tilley and his wife, Roy and his wife, and all the other families on the team made me miss her even more. We ran up enormous phone bills between St. Louis and Portland. We were both looking forward to our impending marriage. "Even though I'm having a good year," I told her, "I need you here." Laurie was more relaxed with our relationship, and I was finally letting her in on my feelings. Telephone love affairs are much harder than people think, but we came incredibly close to each other through those conversations. The wedding plans, her career, the wedding plans, my career, the wedding plans were the typical course of conversation. Surprising her with greeting cards was a great way to use up any extra time I had, and I capitalized on it. They were a lift for Laurie, to let her know that though we were miles apart, she was constantly in my thoughts. Poetry wasn't my forte, but feeling romantic, I'd try my hand at it anyway—mixing my prose with stolen lines from my favorite female singer Amy Grant. The result came out like this:

> Laurie:
> You can thank the Father
> For the things He has done
> And thank Him for the things He's yet to do!
> And if you find a love that's tender
> If you find someone who's true
> Thank the Lord
> He's been doubly good to you.
> And I have found that someone—
> And it is you.
> P.S.—The Lord has been doubly good to both of us. Keep praising His name!

It wasn't Shakespeare, but Laurie liked it!

* * *

The excitement at Busch Stadium was unbelievable. Standing on the sidelines, helmet dangling on my right arm, I squeezed the face mask until my knuckles turned white from pressure. Out on the field, placekicker Neil O'Donoghue was lined up to attempt a 21-yard field goal against the Washington Redskins, who led 24–23. Most of the team watched helplessly, as the 50,262 fans held their collective breath. Even the late-afternoon sun seemed to stop fading over the edge of the stadium, as if it, too, were curious of the outcome.

Sweat trickled down my forehead and I wiped my face with my ever-present towel. The game had been a physical one, and I could feel minor lumps knotting into bruises. In a little over two minutes, we had marched from our own 33-yard line to the Redskins' three, leaving our fate in the hands of O'Donoghue, who unfortunately had often been inaccurate through the season. A victory would mean a first-place tie in the NFC East with Dallas and Washington; a loss would send us plunging back into mediocrity. O'Donoghue had already missed field goals from 34 and 40 yards out, as well as an extra point. Watching a game come down to the kicker wreaks havoc on the old ulcer and is responsible for most gray-headed coaches in the NFL.

I had completed passes of 11, 16, 2, 16, and 21 yards during the final drive. My last pass went to "old reliable" Pat Tilley, who ran a crossing pattern and hung on despite crushing hits from Washington cornerback Darrel Green and free safety Curtis Jordan. Pat's catch set up the field-goal attempt.

The drive culminated an afternoon of some of the best football I'd seen our team play. Four plays into the game, I put up a 38-yard pass resembling the Gateway Arch, which fell between two defenders into the hands of Roy Green. We led at the half, 10–7, and then prevailed in the second half almost in spite of ourselves. We had a punt return for a touchdown called back, and I overthrew Pat Tilley on what could have been a touchdown. The offensive machine of the Redskins, however, was having no such problems, scoring quickly on its first two possessions and taking a 21–10 lead. We maintained our poise, and with little time remaining in the third quarter, I found tight end Doug Marsh for a

19-yard touchdown. On our next possession, the Redskins made their fatal mistake of the day; they tried to cover Roy Green with strong safety Tony Peters, a hard hitter but slow. Roy blazed past him, and I aired it out for an 83-yard touchdown. O'Donoghue could've tied it at 24–24, but missed the point.

Now, every eye in the stadium was focused again on the erratic O'Donoghue. Benny Perrin, our free safety and holder, barked the signals. Every muscle in my body was flexed as I strained to see the action from my sideline perch. My 361 yards passing and three touchdowns would mean nothing to me if we failed to win. "Reaaddddddy," barked Perrin. My stomach felt like a fist; I looked down for a second, almost afraid, but then forced myself to watch. "Huuuuuut." The ball looped back to Perrin; the huge offensive line fired into the Redskins' front wall. O'Donoghue stepped forward, Benny placed the ball, and Neil's foot hit the pigskin. For what felt like eternity, the ball hung suspended in its 21-yard trajectory toward the uprights. I was leaping in expectation.

It tumbled through. The stadium exploded into pandemonium. I turned to face the fans, waving my white towel victoriously with my left hand and indicating "No. 1" with my right hand. Ecstasy, baby. The Cardinals were in first place in the NFC East.

After being emotionally high for three straight weeks, we came down a notch at Philadelphia, but whipped them anyway, 34–14. Although Dan Marino and the Dolphins were stealing the headlines in the AFC, our offense was the talk of the town in the NFC. "The Cardinals are a team with a hot young quarterback, cocky and poised," Paul Zimmerman wrote in *Sports Illustrated.* "He's a guy who won't be intimidated by defenses or screaming fans, and he's operating with offensive linemen who met regularly during the off-season and dedicated themselves to keeping their quarterback upright." Just as much a part of our success was O. J., who Zimmerman called a "master at making the first guy miss, of bleeding yardage out of nothing situations," and Stump

Mitchell, "who either runs away from defenders or splatters them." But our balloon burst the next week, when the Los Angeles Rams snapped our streak with a 16–13 victory on November 16, 1984.

While the pressure was constantly building on me to perform better during the season, the pressure built on all my family members as they sought to cope with "being related to a famous quarterback," according to Mitch. Phone conversations with Mitch always included his telling me how tough it was to live up to, "Hey, your brother is. . . ." It was as though my image as a pro athlete had cast a shadow over the rest of the family, something which I never intended for it to do. But as my national popularity swelled during the course of the season, it was like a blessing with a curse for each family member.

While I had grown accustomed to the media crush, the constant spotlight proved traumatic for my relatives. "Neil, it could destroy my life if I allowed it," Terry told me. "I lose sleep thinking about whether the Cardinals will make the play-offs. I lie awake and think, if you do great, how much more attention will that mean for me? I can't wait to hear the scores of the games. I really thought I was cool just being your brother."

Fortunately, my brothers and sister are keen to the guidance of the Lord, and they made serious efforts not to wear me like a badge. Sometimes my honesty came across as somewhat brutal, but it was very important in my relationship with them to be "Just Neil," not Neil Lomax, St. Louis Cardinals quarterback. Too many athletes who get sucked into the vacuum of superstardom find themselves with nothing after the popularity passes. Ron Kincaid, throughout my youth, had taught me never to put faith in myself. "All things pass away," he'd say. "What will you do then? If you've put your faith in yourself, in your career, what will you do if you're hurt, or if it all ends suddenly?" I emphasized this point to my family.

Mitch and Val never really changed, but during the 1984 season Terry experienced some tough times with my success. He seemed to view it with skepticism, disbelief, and amazement. He admits he allowed it to control him. His personality seemed dependent on whether the Cardinals had won or lost that week. Mitch finally got the point across to Terry.

"Do you know how to tell you're in God's will?" Mitch asked him at mid-season. "Ask yourself, *What is the worst possible situation I could be in?* Then tell yourself that if God told you to go there, you would go." Terry's answer was surprising. "I love the kind of life Neil's career has brought about," he said. "The worst situation I could be in would be for Neil's career to end. I feel special with Neil in the pros."

"That's a fake feeling, and you know it," Mitch told him. "Put your trust, and faith, in God. Not Neil. Neil needs your prayers, not your applause."

Valorie's independence really prevented her from being swayed by the stature of my career. Valorie married Jim Patterson, a stocky, brown-haired good ole Wyoming boy who had played football briefly and is now manager of a Portland radio station. I like Jim; he was the best one for Val. He has really managed to assert himself among the Lomax boys. The toughest part for Valorie is watching me play on television. "I can't stand to watch you get hit," she says. "It really bothers me." It bothers me, too.

Though I was riding high with the Cardinals atop the NFC East at midseason, the sudden attention focused on me had little or no effect on Mitch, who has been the Rock of Gibraltar throughout my tenure in St. Louis. "There's always a temptation to 'show you off' to people," he says. "But knowing Christ is more important than knowing a pro quarterback." Mitch isn't just babbling. Christ has been evident in Mitch's life since his conversion. Mitch was an example. Instead of succumbing to whatever pressure my career success placed on him, he concentrated instead on Christ, setting a spiritual example so high I found it tough to be *his* brother!

Predictably the Dallas Cowboys knocked us out of first place with a 24–17 victory at our place, despite another productive day by our offense. We should've won, but an offensive interference call against Roy Green in the final minute cost us the game-winning touchdown. It was a terrible call. Nevertheless, I played one of my best games of the year, hitting twenty-seven of fifty-two for 388 yards. My totals moved me into the NFL passing yardage lead, ahead of Dan Marino. "The Cardinals are for real," said Dallas head coach Tom Landry. "I was glad to get out of there with a victory." To be mentioned in the same breath with the likes of Joe Montana and Dan Marino was kind of cool, but losing the tough ones had me climbing the walls. Losing, to a quarterback, is a little death, and every loss feels like you're slowly dying. But my anger over the Cowboys loss was nothing compared to what I felt after we lost 16–10 to the New York Giants at the Meadowlands. We had made a habit of going for the big play all season, and the Giants defense put the clamps on. Using Lawrence Taylor as an intimidator—one newspaper described him as "the Boogeyman"—the Giants put on a ferocious pass rush while the linebackers and secondary just laid back waiting for me to throw. Rushed all night, I was intercepted four times and played the worst game of my pro career. The Giants basically did what the Rams did, allowing their linebackers to take deep drops and only let us throw underneath.

I called Laurie that night and cried on her shoulder a little. In the last month, I'd suffered pinched nerves in my shoulder, bruised ribs, and a severe bruise on my elbow. I ached all over. "I miss you, Laurie," I told her. *What a difference it will make,* I thought, *when she can be here all the time.*

The next week Laurie came in for Thanksgiving. Just to see her standing around with the other players and their wives really thrilled me. I beamed with pride as my teammates and their wives got to meet her and was happy with the way she fit in with my Cardinals "family." She felt right at home.

Four teams in the NFC East were competing for the play-offs; us, Dallas, Washington, and the New York Giants, and all four teams, at one time or another during the season, had been in first place. After a horrific November, we edged Philadelphia and then convincingly beat New England and blasted the Giants at home. With one game to play against Washington, who led the division with a 10–5 record, New York and Dallas were tied with us for second place with identical 9–6 records. The entire season had come down to the Redskins: win, and we earned a play-off spot and would be NFL East champions; lose, and we'd go home for the winter.

It was a cold, bitter Washington afternoon, the kind of day when you'd rather curl up in front of a fireplace and read a book than go out tossing footballs into freezing headwinds. A thick mist hung over RFK Stadium and visibility was extremely poor. The surface was loose, muddy, meaning it would be a slow day for receivers and running backs alike.

The game opened miserably, and so many "ifs" ruined our first half. If only linebacker Bob Harris had blocked the Redskins' Rich Mauti on a punt late in the first half. Mauti poured through, blocked the kick, and the 'Skins kicked a cheap field goal. If only O. J. hadn't fumbled to set up Washington's second touchdown. If only the defense could've stopped Joe Theismann, who passed for 192 yards and two touchdowns in two quarters of work. If only I hadn't thrown an interception in the end zone to end the first half. We made countless mistakes, and trailed at the half 23–7. "Dammit, guys. Did we come this far to lose like this?" Hanifan asked at halftime. We hung our heads dejectedly. The coach knew we were on the brink of the play-offs, but seemed lost on how to motivate us. "Anybody who doesn't think we can win this game, then take off your uniform and stay in the locker room," he roared, desperately. "Keep your heads up. Play the second half like it means something." On my way out the door for the second half, Rod gave me a confident wink. "We've got to throw the ball to win, and that's exactly what we're gonna do," he said.

The second half was ours. Starting with short passes to my

running backs, we dinked our way downfield until we forced the Washington cornerbacks to tighten up a little. Neil O'Donoghue hit a 30-yard field goal, a good omen, and on the next series, I figured the defense was ripe for the sting of Roy Green. I took a deep drop, ignored the riot taking place in front of me along the offensive line, and calmly ripped a fastball right across the middle to Roy. He took it in stride, pumping 75 yards for a score. I was brimming with a magical confidence; I knew we could win.

We traded field goals with Washington, and I was confident we could move the ball at will against their defense. With no hesitation, I passed from one side to another—long, short, hard, soft, whatever it took. We were throwing almost every down, but I never gave a single thought to my stats. I wanted to win so bad I could feel a sort of tingling from my toes up through to my shoulders. Heart-grabbing intensity gripped me; on the field, it was as if I were playing in a vacuum, oblivious to the sights and sounds in the packed stands around me. We controlled the line of scrimmage; I dominated the Washington secondary. We were in control, but we were fighting time. Behind 26–29, with 8:45 to play in the game, Roy Green tied Washington cornerback Darrell Green in a knot and broke away cleanly. I singed the cornerback's ears with a high and inside pitch to Roy on a post-corner route, an 18-yard touchdown which capped a 94-yard, six-play drive. For the first time, we led, 27–26. We would win. I sensed it. Tasted it.

But Joe Theismann was equally tough. With his calm, collected, veteran's poise, he battled back. He rescued his team on one third down with a daring scramble, with help from a controversial "roughing the passer" call against E. J. Junior. Two plays later, on third and long, he threaded the needle to receiver Art Monk for 17 yards and another first down. Each time, he barely got the yardage needed. But each time he succeeded. I strapped my helmet on as the darkness settled in around the stadium, the huge rows of lights barely piercing through the haze. The clock kept ticking away. All I wanted was another chance.

Fifty-three yards the Redskins marched, before the drive finally stalled at our 27-yard line with just 1:33 to play. Kicker Mark

Mosely came trotting in off the bench, took a few practice swings, tied his shoe, and punched the ball through with the reliability of a machine. In the face of what could've been disaster, he never flinched. Just boom, field goal. Just like that, we trailed 29–27.

We finally got our last chance, with less than ninety seconds to play and 80 yards between us and the goal line. With every one of the 54,299 Redskins fans yelling at the top of their lungs, we went to work. I utilized virtually every receiver we had, throwing underneath the linebackers for valuable yardage. After four consecutive completions, I threw over Pat Tilley's head to kill the clock. On second down, I hit O. J. Anderson for 1 yard, then Danny Pittman for 5 yards. Suddenly, we were out of downs, timeouts, and almost out of time. With the ball resting on the Redskins' 33-yard line, the field-goal unit came rushing in to squeeze out a last attempt. An attempt of 50 yards.

The thick mist was collapsing onto the field, and I strained from the sidelines to see. Just a few weeks before, O'Donoghue had sunk the Redskins with a last-second kick, but not from this distance. Countless variables rushed through my mind at blazing speed. What if I'd had one more play? What if we could've scored on just one of those wasted opportunities in the first half? Now it had come down to this. Again, I could barely stand to watch. The roar of the Washington crowd made speaking impossible, which was okay, because the lump in my throat would've prevented any sound from coming out. Sweat ran streaks through my dirty face, mud and water dripped off my soaking uniform.

The crowd noise drowned out the cadence of Benny Perrin. Before I could blink, O'Donoghue's leg whipped forward like a spring, and the ball was soaring through the mist, nearly invisible . . . soaring. . . .

Both benches emptied onto the field as players on each side fought for a better view of the ball. Cardinal players all leaned instinctively to their right, in a desperate hope that body language would somehow change the flight of the ball. Oblivious to our actions, however, the ball was hooking left, ever-so-slightly. Too close to tell.

RFK Stadium detonated into bedlam. The ball had missed the

uprights by two feet. I sank to my knees in the mud, still staring into the haze, refusing to believe it was over. Hoping somehow the ball would magically come rewinding back, like in the early black-and-white comedy flicks, and then roll back through the uprights. Washington players were dancing and hugging, fists clenched and helmets raised. We were stunned. Later I would find out I had completed twenty-five of twenty-eight passes in the second half for 314 yards; for the afternoon, thirty-seven of forty-six for 468 yards, the most ever surrendered by the 'Skins. All for nothing. *One more down,* I thought, slamming my helmet into the wet grass. *If only I'd had one more down.*

Our season ended, and the media went wild with my records. My 28 touchdowns in 1984 tied the previous club mark set by Charley Johnson in 1963. My nineteen consecutive games of throwing a touchdown was a club record. The 4,614 yards was a total exceeded only by Dan Marino and Dan Fouts in the history of the NFL. No other Cardinal quarterback had ever come close to either my 92.5 NFL pass rating, or 61.6 percent completion percentage. Four times I eclipsed the 350-yard passing mark, while setting single-game records for completions (37), yards (468), and attempts (52). My efforts were rewarded with a January 1985 trip to the Pro Bowl, the NFL's annual all-star game in Hawaii. Yet, for all the accolades and honors I received, I couldn't erase the sight of Neil O'Donoghue's kick, fading, just barely, to the left of the goalpost. For days all I could think was, *If I'd only had one more down . . . just one more chance.*

When I returned to Portland, everybody was so caught up in preparing for the wedding that my arrival was almost overlooked. Both families were excited. Laurie and I attended seven showers together. There was a Wauna Lake shower, a neighborhood shower . . . the list seemed endless. But we were both so excited we didn't care.

The Pro Bowl was to be held the last weekend in January, and I really wanted Laurie to go with me. Problem was, we weren't getting married until February. I gave Pat Tilley a call and explained the situation. It would be very awkward, especially with my Christian witness, to be introducing "Laurie Exley" in Hawaii, instead of Mrs. Laurie Lomax.

"What do you think I should do, Pat?" I asked. "There's no way I want somebody to think Laurie's just another girl friend. Whether nothing happens or not, nobody would believe me. And, besides, what about Laurie's parents and my parents?"

Pat thought for a second, then made a suggestion.

"Why not have a private ceremony, with just you guys, your parents, and your pastor? Just don't tell anybody, and go ahead and go through with the big ceremony in February."

I liked it. I was determined to take Laurie with me.

"Talk to your pastor, Neil," Pat continued. "I'm sure he'd do it. Big formal weddings are nice, but they're nothing but show. The real ceremony is between you, Laurie, and God." Ron Kincaid agreed.

It went off without a problem. I married Laurie on January 15, played in the Pro Bowl, and two weeks later, enjoyed all the pomp and circumstance of a second, this-time-fancy, unforgettable wedding. It was beautiful. Not only did God give me the girl of my dreams, but he let me marry her *twice*. What a way to cap the biggest year of my career.

11

Passion Play

"A man is only as good as what he loves."

—Saul Bellow

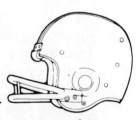

If I'm thankful for anything, it's the fact that Laurie and I founded our relationship over the Bible, instead of over a bottle of beer in a dimly lit nightclub. Our Bible studies throughout 1984 drew us closer together than perhaps anything else, and I could literally feel the two of us being bound together through our love for the Lord.

Laurie's not overbearing; she's not a hit-you-over-the-head-with-my-Bible Christian. Instead, she's an individual who sometimes has a hard time opening up and moves along at her own pace, but feels strongly about her convictions nonetheless. Delving into God's Word creates a sense of togetherness like nothing else can; you can feel yourself and your relationship growing.

But the numbers of people whose relationships are based on spiritual principles are dwindling, which is why I feel a burden to share how important the family really is. Today's permissive attitudes have made it really hard on young men or women just going out into the world. How do we tell a young girl not to fall prey to men when her divorced mother sometimes doesn't come home at night? How do you tell a young man to treat women like ladies when TV's macho men show him otherwise—in his own home—every night? How do we teach our children morals and virtues when everything they see encourages the pursuit of pleasure and instant gratification?

It is more difficult than ever to teach constructive values because of the alarming rejection of Christianity in our society. There exists an entire generation of young people who give no regard to biblical standards. Aaron Hass, a sex researcher for UCLA, revealed recently that 43 percent of boys and 31 percent of girls between the ages of fifteen and sixteen years of age have had sexual intercourse.

In my opinion, there is but one way to combat the problem: by example. Perhaps my answer is too short, too brief, too simple for the doctors, philosophers, and psychiatrists of this world. I'm just a football player, but if playing football has taught me anything, it's that everything takes hard work; there is no instant gratification or success, and if you want to establish yourself as the leader you must work at it and then deserve it. Although my example isn't always perfect, if I can convince one husband, one father, to become a leader in his family, to take charge of his household, then my goal is accomplished.

Don't think it's been easy for me. Making my home in Portland, rather than St. Louis, has made me the subject of public ridicule in St. Louis, but it's something I feel strongly about. I've counted the costs, and it's more important to me to place my wife and my family ahead of my job. To me, the only way that can be done is to separate myself from a situation where I "owe" everybody a part of me. The solitude of Portland, where no one really makes a big deal about me anymore, is important to my homelife. It gives Laurie a sense that I'm hers—she doesn't have to share me with the autograph seekers and picture hounds. Our roots are there, and they're deep. My wife is more important to me than anything, even the professional football team I play for. Our time together is invaluable. It is a great sacrifice of both time and money to maintain shelter and transportation in both cities and to constantly fly two thousand miles, back and forth. But God has given us the means, and I know my priorities. As a leader, I had to put my foot down, regardless of what every broadcaster and sportswriter between Portland and St. Louis thinks about it.

Our Bible studies have often centered around devotions and film series by Dr. James C. Dobson, an expert on marriage and the family. Dr. Dobson once made the point that the way husbands and wives relate is a function of their mutual respect and admiration. That's why marital discord almost always emanates from disrespect somewhere in the relationship. He calls that the "bottom line" of romantic confrontation.

Too many husbands and fathers today, in my opinion, don't take their marital relationships seriously enough. Every season I play in many different cities, often far away from my loved ones and the responsibilities of home. Countless athletes have used their time away to play around, ignoring the damage they were inflicting on their lives.

"Ain't but one problem with messing around," a teammate told me once. "That's if you get caught." Unfortunately, that's the attitude of too many men. You don't have to be a professional athlete, obviously, to cheat on your spouse. Men are not alone. Women are just as tempted by the lure of romanticism. God places a great price on commitment and marriage; and that's a lot to give up simply to satisfy an ego.

When we're told by Christ in Ephesians to love our spouses as He loves the church, there are powerful ramifications to those directions. How does Christ and the church reciprocate love?

Would Christ abuse, ridicule, or downgrade the church? Likewise, the church attaches a great value to Christ. Beautiful, sprawling churches with steeples pointed heavenward are visual monuments to our love for Chirst. In the United States, a great amount of time, money, and effort goes into displaying our public affection for Jesus Christ as witnessed by the number of churches in our nation, representing every denomination. Yet it's exciting to think Christ made all that love and power we feel in a huge, commanding cathedral available on a personal level. A personal relationship with Jesus Christ requires no money, no building, no steeple. And in marriage, that same unconditional love is the glue that binds a husband and wife together. It is the foundation of authentic love.

While studying marriage at a Professional Athletes Outreach Conference, I realized how easy it is to take your spouse for granted. When we first married, my concentration would become so intense during the season that sometimes after a long practice I would sit on the sofa and stare blankly at the television. I wasn't actually watching TV, but going over plays and game situations in my mind. Meanwhile, my wife, who had had a warm dinner waiting for me when I had walked in hours before, was still needing some attention. This frustrated Laurie. Gary Smalley, a Christian relationships counselor, tells a story of a guy who found his wife crying and asked her the problem. "You never tell me you love me anymore," she said. He looked at her and said, "Hey, I told you when I married you. If I change my mind, I'll let you know." That attitude stinks. I wasn't about to let my marriage come to that.

Instead, I began to directly correlate my relationship with Christ to my relationship with Laurie, which is how I feel God intended for it to be. First, I had to admit I was wrong to ignore her, no matter how unintentional it was. I'm forever asking myself, *Would I treat God like that? Would I ignore God?* When we become Christians, do we treat Christ with great respect for only a few years, then give Him the cold shoulder? Like, "Hey,

Jesus, see Ya around, man. I'll come back to You when I get time." During our wedding ceremony, Ron Kincaid told us, "If you're too busy for God, you're too busy. But when you think of your marital and spiritual relationship as one, it makes it so much simpler. Put God first—together. Make your spouse your number one priority—through Christ. Don't neglect Christ for your partner; rather, use your relationship with your partner to become a better Christian."

And God never said marriage had to be boring. There is nothing more exciting to me than to surprise Laurie with a little trip to the lake, a gift, a romantic weekend somewhere, or some other means of letting her know just how special she is in my life. Our married state hasn't kept us from "dating" when schedules permit during the week; if things get too tight, I will make time for her. Too often we get caught up in our careers, and spouses are usually the first to be neglected. But what is success if the person who helped you get there isn't there to share it with you? Our marriage, to me, represents tenderness, openness, and true fairness. Sure, we have problems and disagreements, but never are such incidents more important than we are to each other. Our marriage is like a triangle: Laurie and me on either side, based on a foundation of biblical principles, all pointing upward together in an effort to reach a better understanding of Christ.

Dr. Dobson believes the most successful marriages are those where both the husband and wife seek to build the self-esteem of the other. I certainly agree. In other words, build each other up, instead of taking verbal potshots over problems or trials that may arise. And again, it is the husband who must be the leader.

With divorce running rampant in the United States, it appears to me a decision must be made: either be steamrolled by the problems marriage brings, or love my wife with a reciprocal love, as Christ loves the church. As the leader of my home, I must make the first step. Laurie loves me and is secure in my love for her; she knows football is not the focal point of our relationship. By making the first move, taking the first step, and treating her with the same dignity with which Christ treats the church, I will continue to receive her love in return.

12

The Integrity of the Game

"There is some validity to the union's claims that it is fearful of the players losing their civil rights. But let's face it; in time of war, you have to give up some civil rights."

—Rod Dowhower, head coach,
Indianapolis Colts

Earl Ferrell was entering his fourth year as a running back with the St. Louis Cardinals in 1985 and had reason to believe his best football was ahead of him. The 1985 press guide touted the six-foot, 240-pounder as having "that classic running style . . . he showed us he has breakaway speed and can catch the ball." He could bench press 400 pounds and then outrun a much lighter defensive back. The burning intensity in his eyes was offset by a toothy smile, and his wit and good sense of humor made him a training camp favorite.

But when regular season started that year, Earl wasn't acting right, and that was the first time I had even noticed anything wrong with him. A quarterback is more aware of other players on his unit, and I was noticing subtle changes in Earl. When we watched films he would sit there, as if in a trance, staring straight ahead. He began making mistakes; he was losing his edge of concentration. Earl started forgetting plays, dropping balls, and jumping offsides. The management did nothing.

Team meetings would be interrupted when Earl would duck in late. His speech was occasionally slurred, but his eyes were clear. Then he started missing practices. Management and the coaches quickly shrouded the troubles by putting him on the non-football-related injury list. "Earl Ferrell is having family problems," we were told. What we weren't told is that he had tested positive to cocaine. Once a team has established probable cause concerning drugs, it has the right to test at random. He tested positive again. And again. The second week of the season, Earl Ferrell disappeared. When the starting fullback vanishes, it can make the quarterback and the rest of the offense just a little irritated. We were informed that Earl was out for the year. Gone.

That was the start of a long season for us, and the first time the NFL's growing drug problem in 1985 had really struck home. It wasn't the first time, however, our team had been affected since my arrival.

On April 6, 1982, the same month Earl was drafted, linebacker E. J. Junior had been arrested at a party in Tuscaloosa, Alabama, and charged with possession of cocaine and marijuana. Prosecutors reduced that to a single-felony charge of narcotics possession. E. J. played the entire 1982 season under bond. In February of 1983, he was sentenced to two years probation and Commissioner Pete Rozelle suspended him for four weeks, which meant E. J. forfeited $30,000 in salary. Junior's dilemma shook up several guys on the team, but he not only straightened out his act, he also started counseling patients in the adolescent drug and alcohol abuse program at St. Louis's Care Unit Hospital.

But Junior's experience didn't teach Earl Ferrell anything. Through Earl, cocaine again gripped our team, and it tightened its hold as the season wore on. Earl was obviously not the only guilty party. Late in the year the management, growing paranoid from all the horror stories floating around the league, surprised us with a random drug test, which was strictly against the collective bargaining agreement held by our union, the National Football League Players Association. As union members, all but seven of my teammates refused to take the test. Mr. Bidwill fined us $1,000 for our display of solidarity and threatened to get rid of us all. Drugs weren't the only reason we suffered through a 5–11 season, but it created bad feelings between the management and the team, separated the coaching staff, and ignited arguments among the players themselves.

During the 1985 season, I realized what a horrible drug cocaine really is. It rendered a strong, powerful fullback like Earl Ferrell helpless. Then it totally disintegrated any unity the Super Bowl runner-up New England Patriots might have had. I was relieved to see the season end, but it didn't stop there. Cocaine continued to crawl like a serpent through the nation, choking life from Maryland basketball player Lenny Bias and Cleveland Browns' safety Don Rogers.

Still shocking to me is that our union and NFL management continue to use random drug testing as a toehold for negotiations. More shocking is that it took the deaths of Len Bias and Don Rogers to get Commissioner Pete Rozelle to recognize the problem. Professional football is beginning to stink from within, and two main issues burn on my conscience.

First, the NFL must quit thinking about the scoreboard and start thinking about players' lives. Too many drug problems get pushed under the rug because a particular player plays a big part in Sunday's outcome. Team officials must crack down on all drugs. Drugs are drugs. There is no gray area. That means anabolic steroids and even alcohol abuse. Jack Lambert, a former Pittsburgh linebacker, hit the drug issue harder than he used to hit quarterbacks: "We talk about how bad cocaine is, but we turn the other cheek when it comes to steroids," he says. "That, to me, is hypocrisy at its highest." I agree. There should be an equal amount of education incorporated with random drug testing. Not one without the other.

Second, teams must recognize the pressure involved in professional sports. Cocaine is just one obvious problem that has resulted from the pressure of asking twenty-one-year-old men to be the heroes of an entire society. Certainly, we chose to play this game, but teams have a responsibility to help players cope and to work harder at educating the professional athlete when such needs arise. Don't wait for the ailment to treat the symptom; treat the source before there is ever a flare-up.

For too many years, the drug problem was ignored in the National Football League. With every new television contract, with every new multimillion-dollar stadium, with every new Super Bowl trophy, Pete Rozelle continued to harp on how "the integrity of the game" was holding fast. At every opportunity, Rozelle preached that the league was at its best, that the public was gaining a newfound confidence in this great American sport we call pro football. Likewise, Gene Upshaw, executive director of the National Football League Players Association, said his purpose was to uphold the integrity of the game, and the integrity of the players' rights.

The real Pete Rozelle shone through after Super Bowl XX when someone asked him what he would do about the drug problem. "What drug problem?" he asked. ". . . we just got a 40-plus Nielsen rating for the Super Bowl, and you're asking about drugs?" Thanks Pete. Five months after those profound words, the family of Don Rogers lowered his casket six feet into the earth. If there's anything I'm sick of, it's watching the public get snowed by the NFL's first-rate public relations department.

Gene Upshaw and our union are far from innocent. When the drug issue arose, we were under the collective bargaining agreement hammered out in 1982. That agreement contained no specific penalties for drug use, leaving discipline to the discretion of Rozelle. Until people started dying, Rozelle ignored the problem.

Public reaction forced him to do something. Although his "something" might have been a knee-jerk reaction to the death of Rogers, it was a start.

Rozelle proposed a "master" plan that would subject all NFL players to two surprise urinalysis tests during the season. The unannounced tests were part of a comprehensive plan the commissioner unveiled to "preserve the integrity of the game," he said. There he goes again. C'mon, Pete, cut out the "integrity of the game" crap. Right now, there isn't any integrity. First, clean up the game, then talk about its integrity.

Upshaw reacted to Rozelle's plan like a cat tossed into a swimming pool. He was violently opposed to it. "I think the NFL and Pete Rozelle are trying to make a grandstand play," he said. "We plan to take all steps necessary to protect the rights of the players."

First, let me say I had no choice about being a union member. You are automatically inducted when you sign an NFL contract. My union membership costs me around $2,500 a year in dues, which are automatically deducted from my paychecks. As a union member, however, I do feel a responsibility to act with the union, even going out on strike, although I don't always agree with it. In the instance of random drug testing, I vehemently disagree with the union.

Gene Upshaw makes random testing a matter of civil rights and uses it in his negotiations with the NFL. That's the stupidest thing I've ever heard of. This isn't a matter of salaries, a matter of free agency, or a matter of negotiations. Human lives are at stake. Somebody tell Don Rogers about his civil rights.

While random testing can't save lives, it can reveal existing problems. Certainly, we need our civil rights in this society. But as professional athletes before a nation of impressionable kids and teenagers, we have a responsibility to set an example, whether we like it or not. We get paid a lot of money to play football, so how bad can it hurt to bend our rights just a little in this case? We should be leaders. Drugs are a pervasive problem, and when players make more headlines for drug abuse than football ability, it adds fuel to the fire. If we have to prove our innocence to set an example, then we should. I urinate every day anyway, so if management wants it, what's the big deal?

Yet the union insists on using the matter of testing as leverage, ignoring the fact that drugs are also illegal. Suppose NFL players were stealing cars? Would the union strike a deal that would allow us to steal a car once, be warned, steal another, be warned, and then finally sent to a Car Stealing Rehabilitation Center for a month? The union wants to limit drug testing to twice a year. How about two stolen cars a year? Just two, no more. That is no more ridiculous than the union's ideas.

There is one glaring problem with Rozelle's drug plan, which will cost owners $1 million annually if implemented. Rozelle only calls for thirty-day suspensions and mandatory hospitalizations for some first-time offenders; sixty-day suspensions without pay for second-time offenders; and at least a one-year ban for third-time offenders.

I think first-time offenders should be suspended; second-time offenders should be banished. Period. We don't need drug users in the NFL any more than we need car thieves or murderers. Is it right for athletes who are admitted drug users to be exonerated, while thousands of people across the country are arrested and prosecuted? I'm sick of the double standard that favors pro athletes. We're spoiled enough already. The only reason the NFL wants to protect us and provide rehabilitation is that we are part of a big business and represent a major source of revenue.

Young men are dying. The National Institute on Drug Abuse estimates there are now close to 6 million cocaine users in the United States, consuming over forty-five metric tons of the powder every year. The number of deaths by cocaine intoxication, meanwhile, has tripled since 1983. We in professional sports owe it to the paying public to set an example.

The education process must start in the schools, particularly the colleges. Too many kids are sucked in by fast-talking agents who use dope to bait their clientele. I've spoken at colleges where some guys were majoring in sports and playing education. The stark facts must be presented, not only about drugs, but how few players ever make it to the pros. In 1985, 1 million kids played high school football in the United States; only 48,634 played college football, less than 6 percent of the high school total. Only 1 in 5,000 of the best high school stars will ever see the National Football League. That should be motivation to end the pipe dream of a big-time sports career. Students should be urged to think education first, sports second.

Get the coaches involved. If a college player gets caught with drugs, ban him from the team for the next season. I don't care if he's the Heisman Trophy winner.

We will never have a drug-free society. Incidents will always arise. But we must not ignore it any longer.

When E. J. Junior rebounded from drugs, he was very honest as to what started him downhill, what made him look for answers in that soft white liar called cocaine. "I had free time, a lot of money, and a lot of curiosity," he says. "And that means trouble. It doesn't take long to lift weights in the off-season, maybe three hours a day. That leaves twenty-one hours to get into trouble. We've got to educate players what to do with their money and their time . . . it's a real trap. There's so much pressure involved with the game today."

Ah, *pressure*. The magic word. Pro football is a business, and everybody is making money off this business, so problems that otherwise would be treated with care get brushed over in sports to allow business to continue. Brushed over because we, the "heroes," are the same larger-than-life warriors who put the points on the board each Sunday for the entertainment of countless thousands. Drugs are one issue; pressure is another. Everyone doesn't succumb to drugs. But we all, in some way, feel the pressure.

Desite our God-given abilities, nobody makes us become pro athletes. We chose this career. But the freewheeling, pressure-packed life-style can overwhelm you and the result is disastrous. Young men, many of whom were raised in the ghettoes of America's cities, suddenly have tremendous wealth, and as E. J. said, lots of free time. To ease the pressure, some turn to drugs.

Others blow money on cars or clothes. The love of money, and the craving for more, is doing as much to destroy the NFL as drugs. The players' greed only parallels that of the owners.

Fans envision every player making $1 million a year, taxfree, and think we never have problems, we get free televisions and cars, and everybody plays fourteen or fifteen years like Roger Staubach or O. J. Simpson. Then, after retirement, we all get tryouts for the ABC "Monday Night Football" crew.

I hate to shatter the dream, but this is a hard business. It takes a special-caliber person to handle the pressure. We're humans; we all make mistakes. We face the same personal problems that everyone else does. We have wives and families and children. We have mortgages and phone bills and car payments. We also have the media publicizing our every move.

Pro ball isn't a picnic. The joy of throwing a touchdown and seeing a little boy's face light up is still very real to me. The game itself is still a lot of fun, or I would get out. It's the ramifications brought on by the game that make it tough. Society places us high on a pedestal, as if we're superhuman. Statistics, however, sing a different song. Virtually 70 percent of all professional athletes have been divorced or separated. After the Kansas City Chiefs won the 1970 Super Bowl, they were lauded as "the team of the future." Today, 69 percent of the team of the future is divorced.

The pressure is constant; it eats at you spiritually, mentally, and physically. First, the homelife erodes, and marriages are usually the first casualty. For some taking drugs is a way to cope with the pressure. Still others spend their evenings in bars, sipping on a bourbon and water to numb their senses and fend off the demons that aggravate their minds.

With few exceptions, players never seem to think about the day their careers will end. They come to training camp thinking they'll always be able to do it again next year. It's very hard for an athlete to admit to himself that someday he will not be able to run as fast, to tackle as hard, or to throw as far as he did the year before. There's always "next year," as in, "I'll play better next year," or, "I'll get a bigger contract next year," or, "I'll get rid of my drug problem next year." The problem touches both ends of the spectrum. Jim Hart, whose only problem was the passing of time, couldn't face "next year." Don Rogers never saw "next year."

The day I scrawled my name on a professional contract, my life changed. No longer referred to as "Neil," I became "Neil Lomax, the quarterback for the St. Louis Cardinals." Neil Lomax, the superstar, the million-dollar baby. People think just because we make the money, we travel all over the country, and everyone wants our autograph that we've got it made. They don't see the silver-tongued "friends" who want to help manage our money, or the investment brokers who take $5,000 downpayments and never return. They don't see the paranoia that comes when everybody wants a piece of you. They don't see us changing our phone numbers every two weeks to keep the media and irate fans from bothering us at all hours of the night. The game has left deep scars on many players, some of whom never touched a drug in their lives.

Tony Dorsett, for instance, prior to signing a renegotiated contract in 1985, not only had paychecks garnished by the IRS, but also had liens placed on his two homes. It was reported at the time that he owed $414,277.91 in back taxes. Tony's divorce, which took place only months before his IRS troubles, cost him $250,000 and a 1981 Mercedes. Tony took an unfair whipping by the media when his problems became public, but he was only one of many who play for years and suddenly find themselves with nothing. Fortunately, the Cowboys rescued him financially. Tell Tony how "easy" it is to be a professional football player.

Players should be better educated in college. Athletes with failing grades who are allowed to play anyway should be a thing of the past. Any potential draft pick or free agent—in any sport—should be taught about the hyped-up promises of agents, the basics of the standard player's contract, and all the dangers that await them. Learning to handle the pressure should be a subject every college coach tackles with his players, and athletes should be taught to move slowly, use their heads, and think for a change. Don't rush. Don't talk to everybody who seems friendly.

Don't go to "those" parties just because you're Big Man on Campus. Thank God I had people like Mouse Davis, Ron Kincaid, and Mitch to keep me out of most "situations."

Too much emphasis is placed on the shiny cars, fast women, and beer commercials which have become synonymous with professional sports. The glamour of worldliness has its appeal, but I can't forget the words of Ecclesiastes 11:9, which Ron Kincaid pointed out to me ten years ago. "Rejoice, O young man, in thy youth; and let thy heart cheer thee in the days of thy youth, and walk in the ways of thine heart, and in the sight of thine eyes: but know thou, that for all these things God will bring thee into judgment." That was all I needed to hear.

Indeed, the game of football has brought me fame. But when my career is through, I don't want to be remembered for being a great guy. I'd rather be remembered for having a great God. Religion isn't the answer to the problems we've outlined, but having a personal, day-to-day relationship with Jesus Christ has made it possible for me to cope. Instead of trying drugs or other "unnatural" highs to cure your problems, try Jesus. I don't have all the answers, and I don't pretend to. It's not the integrity of the game that motivates me; rather, the integrity of knowing God.

E. J. Junior found out in time. I know Earl Ferrell did, too. It rips at my stomach, however, to think of the young people who are finding out too late.

Epilogue:
New Beginnings

"Neil will be a great father. He's patient, loving and tender. Most of all, because of his leadership, our children will have strong Christian values. The way Neil shares time and love with his dog every day is proof of how he will treat his kids. He's a loving man, a truly loving husband."

—Laurie Lomax

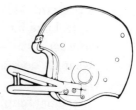

No one was surprised when Jim Hanifan and his entire staff got the boot immediately after we lost to Washington to end the dismal 1985 season. The funniest thing was that the coaching staff was let go instantly after the game, and when they returned to their offices to clean out their desks, they couldn't unlock the doors. Can you believe management had changed the locks to all the doors—*during* the game?

But those days are over. The hiring of new head coach Gene Stallings, a longtime Dallas assistant, brings new hopes for the future. Stallings, a tall man with graying dark hair and a rugged face, is a disciplinarian; kind of a cross between Paul "Bear" Bryant and Don Shula. Either way, in my opinion, you have a winner. The "flat tire" and "overslept" excuses that plagued the Hanifan regime will be nonexistent under Coach Stallings. A disciple of such coaching legends as Tom Landry and the Bear, Stallings is a firm family man who forms his own conclusions. No longer is there any question as to who is in charge. Nor is there any doubt he knows how to win. Jim Shofner, my fourth quarterback coach in six years, came along with Stallings from the Dallas system.

"Everyone starts with a clean slate," Stallings told us at mini-camp at Busch Stadium in May 1986. "That's why I didn't keep any of the coaches from last year. I didn't want to hear any negative comments from them about the players. If there are problems, I'll find them myself. And I will get rid of them myself."

It appears Coach Stallings will be able to revive the potential that led experts to pick us as Super Bowl contenders after 1984. He stressed continually his goal of making the play-offs, and that old, confident feeling the team had been developing two years ago started sneaking back. His forwardness will be good for the team; he even managed to scare Joe Bostic, our big, surly offensive guard. "He sure is honest," Joe said after our first mini-camp. "I feel like I'm in the military. It's fantastic, really. I'm not going to wear a ball cap or chew tobacco or anything until I find out what he does and doesn't like. Right now, the man has my respect."

Similar sentiments were expressed by most of the other players, which was a big surprise when compared to former coaching staffs. When we opened training camp July 17, the largest number of players in club history reported. Coach Stallings urged Mr. Bidwill, the owner, to bring a large number of free agents to camp to increase competition for roster spots. In another unprecedented move, Mr. Bidwill did what a coach asked *him* to do, instead of the other way around. That also went a long way in winning the respect of the players. "It's important to create the best competitive environment possible at training camp," Coach Stallings said. "I think it can make a difference for us." Other changes were rapidly evident under our new coach. He demanded a sorely needed weight facility and new office space at the stadium, and he got it. "I know discipline is important to have a championship football team," he told us. "I don't think there's any way we can have a championship team without it. But most of discipline is self-discipline. I can want it, but you guys have to want it. I will help you want it."

Proof of Coach Stallings's leadership came quickly, in only our fourth exhibition game of the 1986 season. We were playing the Super Bowl Champion Bears at Chicago when the contest turned into a barroom brawl. Referee Pat Haggerty and his crew of officials really let the game get out of hand in the first half. The Bears' defense, which thrives on its "nasty" reputation, dished out far too many late hits. In the second quarter, William "the Refrigerator" Perry viciously slammed me to the ground with an obvious cheap shot; Joe Theismann said later that Perry should've been "at least fined, possibly suspended." The tension exploded when a bench-clearing fight broke out in the third quarter.

Livid, Coach Stallings threatened to take us off the field. Haggerty informed him he would face ramifications from Pete Rozelle and the NFL if he did. "You worry about your job and I'll worry about mine," Stallings told Haggerty with gritted teeth. "I'm doing what I think's right for the protection of my players." We won, 14–7, and physically whipped the "awesome" Bears. And Coach Stallings won our respect and confidence like never before.

I'm excited. That old feeling is back.

This fall, Laurie will give birth to our first child. We are looking forward in great expectation and have prepared ourselves carefully for the task of child rearing that lies ahead. Soon the examples we set will be more crucial than ever; the lessons we've learned through the years will serve as our foundation. As Ron Kincaid told us, "Just because both of you are Christians doesn't mean your kids will be." Football games are often won or lost in the hands of a receiver. Passes that could win games are often dropped, and however great the play might have been, it is quickly forgotten.

Thus, as we prepare to pass along spiritual concepts to our child, I realize that "pass" will be the most critical of my career. I might add, too, that I won't be happy with anything short of the goal line.